The Amazing World of American Birds

About the Book

In this book the noted nature writer Lucille Wood Trost describes in vivid detail the surprising lives of a great variety of American birds. Here are strange, true stories of inland gull colonies, of golden eagles that kill only when hungry, of the tiny ruby-throated hummingbird that flies 500 miles over open seas. The distinguished natural history artist Joseph Sibal illustrates with superb drawings Mrs. Trost's account of a bird world that will amaze readers with its variety and richness of experience.

MARSH BIRDS *(Clockwise from bottom)* Long-billed Marsh Wren, Savannah Sparrow, Red-eyed Vireo, Seaside Sparrow, Sharp-tailed Sparrow

The Amazing World of American Birds

by Lucille Wood Trost

illustrated by Joseph Sibal

G. P. PUTNAM'S SONS, NEW YORK

To my husband, Chuck—for his warm encouragement, helpful
comment and infectious love of birds
and
To my son, Scott—for his questions, suggestions, and the sharing
of his bird-filled life

Contents

FLIGHTLESS BIRDS (*Top left*) Diatryma (prehistoric), (*top right*) Moa (extinct), (*bottom from left to right*) Ostrich, Emu, Rhea, Cassowary

1
The Order of Things

On the open dry plains of Africa live the world's largest birds: 8 feet tall, about 317 pounds, unable to fly but capable of running 30 miles per hour. If cornered, an ostrich can slash open the belly of a lion with two-toed, heavily clawed feet.

With gnu, antelope, and zebras move groups of ten to fifteen ostriches. The movement of these grazing groups disturb the smaller creatures of the land; insects, rodents, reptiles try to flee. But the ostriches feed easily on these creatures disturbed by the grazers—and in turn they benefit their fellow travelers. The long ostrich necks stretch high above the other animals, eyes sharp and alert. They spot lions hunting in the tall grass or humans creeping with guns, and their behavior warns their feeding companions.

Off the coast of the southeastern United States on the island of Cuba live the world's smallest birds. The Cuban bee humingbird is about the size of a large bumblebee and about equal in weight to a dime. Brilliant red and green in color, gemlike, a master of flight, this tiny bird can move its wings up to 200 beats a second. It can hover like a helicopter, move forward or backward, up, down, sideways, and stop or start with extreme suddenness.

Ostriches and hummingbirds, bluebirds, gulls, wrens, owls, chickadees, eagles, geese, ducks, sandpipers, woodpeckers, pelicans—there are many, many kinds of birds. There are about 8,600 living species. About 645 of these are found in North America. Some are large, some small. Some live in water, others on deserts. Some stay to the thick enclosure of woodland; some move freely in the open sky. Some have long slender bills; those of others are thick and heavy. The only place birds have not been found is in the center of the year-round deeply frozen Antarctic.

Scientists place all birds in the class of animals called Aves. There is a very simple way to divide members of this group from all others. *Birds are animals with feathers.* No animal without feathers is a bird. No animal with feathers is anything but a bird.

It seems an easy jump from feathers to flight. We might ask, "Are birds feathered animals that fly?" No. As we have seen from the ostrich, not all birds fly. Yet connecting flight with birds is not very far from the truth. Even flightless birds had ancestors that flew, and all birds have bodies that are *adapted* or fitted for flight. The characteristics that they share in addition to feathers reflect this fact. All birds have forelimbs modified into wings. Their hind limbs are used for walking, swimming, or perching. No living bird has teeth. Avian skeletons are very light with many parts fused or grown together. All birds also have a four-chambered heart, air sacs throughout the body, the ability to regulate a high body temperature, and they lay eggs. These traits are important for flight.

Many of the avian specialties may be found in other animals. All mammals have a four-chambered heart and the ability to regulate their temperatures. Both apes and humans have hind legs adapted for walking; the hind legs of seals and walruses are made for swimming. Reptiles, fish, and amphibians all lay eggs. Bats have their forelimbs modified for flying. When all the characteristics of birds are considered together, however, there is no other animal that has them all.

In order fully to understand the place of birds among animals, we have to look at two fields of scientific understanding: taxonomy and evolution.

Taxonomy is a science that attempts to arrange or classify plants and animals according to their relationships to other living things. Before the eighteenth century animals and plants were grouped in very crude and superficial ways. People believed all creatures had been created separately, so it was pointless to look for relationships between them. They classified living things as the dog kind, the cat kind, or the bird kind, and for specific animals only common names such as chickadee or crow were used. A great deal of confusion arose this way. Common names were not exact enough for scientific purposes, and they differed from place to place. In addition, they told nothing of the structure or relationships of the animal or plant. We can still see this today. The

8

"four and twenty blackbirds baked in a pie" are not the type of bird we in the United States might imagine. European blackbirds are really thrushes, as are our robins. In behavior, appearance, and internal structures these birds differ greatly from the scientific classification of blackbirds.

In the eighteenth century a man named Carolus Linnaeus was bothered by the problem of scientifically talking about animals and plants. Linnaeus decided to create a better system by giving all living things a two-part scientific name. Now we say a species is all those living things that can breed together. Linnaeus simply described a species as a group of living creatures that were very much alike.

Now it is relatively easy to learn scientific names and to fit them to various plants and animals. You need only a good taxonomy book, a magnifying instrument of some type, sharp eyes, and patience. It's even fairly easy to classify a new animal by comparing its characteristics to published descriptions and deciding where it belongs. In this way one or two bird species and many thousands of insects are discovered and named every year.

The job was far from simple in Linnaeus' day, however. He did not know that all animals and plants truly were related to one another over time. Yet he was not content randomly to assign each plant and animal a name. He saw similarities and differences among groups of animals. It seemed possible to divide types at many levels. For example, plants and animals were both living things but there were great differences between them too. Thus he set up two kingdoms: plant and animal. This process of dividing on the basis of similarities and differences he continued downward to smaller and smaller groupings. In this manner he created the ideas of kingdom, phylum, class, order, and family. Before his work was finished, Linnaeus had a very large task indeed.

Today scientists agree that all living things have come into being by a process called evolution. Life began in the shallow warm ocean waters billions of years ago. By accident a group of chemicals came together. A bolt of lightning probably united them. So was life born—possibly many times—a very tiny thing, and it was neither plant nor animal. From such simple beginnings have arisen all living things.

The creation of the first life was a very great change for the earth, of course, but there is another part of equal importance. The first living bit did not remain as it began. In some way it reproduced itself. As its numbers grew, it spread away from the place where it had begun. The oceans were not the same all over. The shallow warm waters and the deep cold areas of dark were not equally hospitable to the first living things. Many of those that moved away from the place of beginning died, but some did not. Most of the survivers in the new places were slightly different from their ancestors. They reproduced themselves and spread farther.

In time there arose many different living things. Life moved onto land. It moved into air. It continued spreading and changing. On land, in the air, or in the water, the living things that survived were always the ones best suited to a particular way of life. They produced the most offspring that resembled themselves.

The earth is a restless planet, however. Mountains rose. Glaciers moved southward, then retreated again. The air was cold, then hot, then cold again. Rivers cut downward into newly uplifted plains. New life places were formed constantly, and old species were wiped out. In this manner there came into being all those many very different plants and animals we know today. The steady selection of those that fit each place best has continued for billions of years. It continues today. The great variety of birds shows the results of adaptation and evolution very clearly.

Linnaeus did not know about evolution, however, and this increased his problem greatly. There were so many traits he might study. For birds alone, which should he use for his classification system: Size? Color? Bill shape? Foot structure? Eye placement? Wing shape? Courting behavior? Nest? The list could go on for pages.

If he looked at beak shape alone, for example, he would place together many birds that scientists have now agreed are separate. Hummingbirds would fit with shorebirds. Hawks and owls would be classified together. Ornithologists—scientists who study birds—now know that such a classification is not correct. The bill shape is only a specialization for feeding. It tells little more. Other parts of modern classification do not make sense at all when we look at them superficially. Ostriches, rheas, and emus look very much alike but are placed in different groups called orders. Loons and grebes also resemble each other, yet are in different orders. Conversely, cranes and coots do not seem at all similar in appearance, yet are placed together. Such problems are easily explained from the scientist's point of view.

Our modern taxonomic classification is different from that of Linnaeus. It can be represented as a picture of a tree of evolution with many highly forked branches. Some of the branches are still growing. Others are dead or extinct. Scientists no longer rely on easily changed superficial characteristics to understand such evolutionary relation-

10

ships. Instead, they consider the internal anatomy such as skeleton, muscles, or the form of the foot. There is far from total agreement on the places of all birds, however, and classification systems often vary. Some modern taxonomists have changed our understanding of relationships by studying the chemistry of blood and egg proteins.

Let's look more closely at taxonomy by classifying a bird we all know.

Kingdom: Animal.   All birds have some traits in common with all other animals but not with plants. Animals have a nervous system and the ability to move from place to place. They must get their food from other living things. Plants do not have a nervous system and are attached throughout life. They make their own food.

Phylum: Vertebrata.   All birds are animals with backbones. They share this trait with amphibians, fish, reptiles, and mammals.

Class: Aves.   The feathered animals.

Order: Passeriformes.   The perching birds—the largest and evolutionarily most recent group. There are 5,100 species in 55 families. Three-fifths of the world's birds are passerines.

Family: Turdidae.   The thrushes. Many with spots on the breasts of young or adults.

Genus: *Turdus.*

Species: *migratorius.*

Scientific name: *Turdus migratorius.*

Common name: American robin.

There are 27 orders and 155 families of birds in the world today, and 17 orders are found in the United States. It is the latter 17 orders we will consider in this book.

2
The Orders of Birds

1. Gaviiformes—Loons

2. Podicipediformes—Grebes

3. Pelecaniformes—Pelicans, anhingas, and cormorants

4. Anseriformes—Waterfowl

5. Falconiformes—Hawks, vultures, and falcons

6. Galliformes—Chickenlike birds

7. Ciconiiformes—Herons and their allies

8. Gruiformes—Cranes and rails

9. Charadriiformes—Shorebirds, gulls, terns, auks

10. Columbiformes—Pigeons and doves

11. Cuculiformes—Cuckoos and roadrunners

12. Strigiformes—Owls

13. Caprimulgiformes—Goatsuckers

14. Apodiformes—Swifts and hummingbirds

15. Piciformes—Woodpeckers

16. Coraciiformes—Kingfishers

17. Passeriformes—Perching birds

12

3
Ancient Wings

In a slate quarry in Bavaria in 1861 the imprint of a living thing was found. Embedded in the rock was a lizardlike feathered creature never seen before. Rumors spread rapidly. The theory of evolution had just been stated. Had a missing link been found? Was there some new proof for this strange and frightening theory that said all living things had come into being from a common beginning?

Many scientists came to study the find. At first they were puzzled and suspicious. Could this strange new creature be a practical joke? In many ways it was very much like a reptile, yet it had feathers. The idea of a practical joke soon was abandoned. Specialists who study the age of the earth's rocks came to see the specimen. They agreed it was very old. The layer of the earth in which it had been found was ancient. The rock was formed during a time period called Jurassic about 150,000,000 years ago.

Carefully biologists noted the traits of the strange new crow-size creature. It was perfectly preserved with the head twisted back in an S curve; wings and tail flopped out. Both bones and feathers easily were seen. It had a lizardlike head and toothed jaws. There was a long, slender, bony tail. The feathers were linked to it, one pair per bone, all the way to the end. It had abdominal ribs like reptiles and wings with claws at the bend. Yet it flew, and the shoulder girdle, pelvis, and legs were similar to those of modern birds. At last scientists decided the new creature was a bird extinct long ago. They called it *Archaeopteryx* which means "ancient wing."

Today, more than one hundred years since this first most ancient skeletal bird was found, we think we have a good picture of *Archae-*

13

opteryx and its world. This ancient animal was not really very much like modern birds in its behavior. It had no graceful spiraling flight and could not execute swift sweeps and turns. It captured very little food on the wing. Flying insects and the faster animals living on land could easily escape its gliding. Gigantic blue-glistening dragon-flies of the time, with their six-foot wingspans and swift, darting flight, made a mockery of *Archaeopteryx's* claim to the air. This ancient bird was a poor flier. It is fairly certain it simply glided on outstretched wings groundward from treetops, much as do flying squirrels today. *Archaeopteryx* spent a fair amount of time on the ground, and it was well suited for this life also. If danger threatened, it could escape easily. Its legs were strong and could run swiftly. With the aid of the clawed wings it scrambled back to the tops of trees.

Yet even poor flight gives an advantage to those that possess it. The high-swaying treetops were safer than the ground; there were almost no enemies, and approaching danger was spotted easily. If necessary, one could escape quickly by gliding to another tree or the ground. An animal in such a situation did not need to remain silent and hidden. Perhaps in this early safety the seeds for birdsong and bright coloration were planted. *Archaeopteryx* could give its harsh cry while safe from predators; it could puff out its brilliant red featherless throat pouch, and in these ways it could attract a mate. A ground-dwelling animal could not afford to be so obvious.

The world beneath the palmlike trees in which *Archaeopteryx* perched was very different from the one we know today. The climate was mild. Thick, low carpetings of ferns and horsetails spread over the earth. There were no flowering plants or grasses, and most of such modern trees as oak, maple, and poplars were missing. Most trees were of the palmlike type called cycads, although there were some tree ferns and evergreens. There were many living things that did resemble the modern, although a closer look would have shown they were different. There were ants, wasps, beetles, bees, crickets, worms, and amphibians. The first small primitive mammals had appeared. They gave birth to hairless, helpless young and busily fed on the roots of ferns. The seas were filled with corals, jellyfish, oysters, sea urchins, snails, and bony fish.

These familiar creatures would not be the most obvious life forms to visitors from other times, however. *Archaeopteryx* lived in the age of reptiles, and these scaled creatures were everywhere in great numbers. They were on the land as the largest of dinosaurs. The meat eater *Allosaurus* and the slow, heavy plant eater *Brontosaurus* both lived

14

(*Top left*) Ramphorynchus, a flying reptile, (*center*) Archaeopteryx, (*bottom right*) Pterodactylus

during the Jurassic. Reptiles were in the seas. Some had paddles for legs and long snakelike necks. Others looked very much like long-snouted toothy fish. Reptiles were also in the air. As they fed, they darted and glided over land and sea very much as swallows do today. These flying creatures were called pterodactyls. They had narrow wings of stretched skin membranes and long, flattened tails with strange leaflike attachments at the end. There is no doubt that pterodactyls were reptiles, but they had many birdlike features such as light bones and beaks. Such traits would be necessary to move through the air. The reptile flying experiment died out about 63,000,000 years ago.

It may seem strange that birds began during the time of reptiles, yet it fits beautifully with what we know from the fossil record. During the age of reptiles there were roughly two classes of dinosaurs: the lizard hips and the bird hips. The bird hips walked upright and had front legs specialized for use in handling food. It is from this group that birds probably came. The thecodonts were small dainty dinosaurs that ran rapidly and semi-erectly on long hind limbs. The tail was used for balance. They may very well have been part of the line that led to birds.

If we drew an evolutionary tree, a branch would jag off from the lifeline that led to mammals. Farther on, the branch would again fork. One portion leads to modern reptiles, the other to birds. The two lines moved apart about 150,000,000 years ago, shortly after the first mammals had appeared.

The relationship between birds and reptiles is so close that one well-known biologist said that birds are simply glorified reptiles. Scientists group the two together into a superclass called Sauropsida. They share many bone and muscle features and have very similar eggs. The young of both groups have an egg tooth for chipping out of the shell. Birds have scales on the legs, and reptiles are sheathed with these strong flattened waterproof coverings. In addition, feathers are only modified forms of the scales of lizards and snakes. The chemical composition is the same, and the stages of development are similar.

Imagine a trip through time to the Cretaceous period. It is 100,-000,000 years ago. A warm clear sea stretches away from a rocky shore. Beneath these waters lies the land that someday will be called Kansas. It will be a place of dry farms with only potholes of freshwater in which ducks breed, a land of sunflowers, straight cuts of road, and large neat farmhouses. But long ago there was no hint of this.

The inland sea moves smoothly with its tidal flow. Frothy waves

EXTINCT WATERBIRDS (*Bottom left*) Ichthyornis, (*bottom right*) Hesperornis

crash on the curving shore. There are small rocky islands dotting the wide sweep of waters. This is the home of two ancient birds: *Hesperornis* and *Ichthyornis*. It is also the home of many of the other creatures that we met in the Jurassic times. Fishlike reptiles slide long-necked and glistening through the seas. Pterodactyls still glide about in the air and swoop close to the waters in fishing. The land plants and reeds are similar to those of the Jurassic. They still would be strange to us.

Walking quietly along the shore, one comes to a sheltered cove. Hide among the tall, filmy ferns and slender, firm bodies of horsetails, and watch a moving glitter on the waters. Not far from shore there is a group of about fifteen birds. They seem relaxed and almost sleepy. A few preen themselves by touching a large oil gland on the back, then spreading the released liquid to the feathers. A strange deep call floats back and forth: *Huookuuh . . . huookunk.*

If you watch closely, you may notice a strong resemblance to a bird

17

you know. The tapering body, long, slender neck, thin bill, upright head, and high floating posture are all familiar. These birds strongly resemble the modern loons of northern lakes—yet they are not. There are obvious differences of color and size. The wings are small and incapable of flight, besides other less obvious differences. These are *Hesperornis*—a type of bird long extinct.

Suddenly the quiet scene changes. A shoal of silvery fish erupts from the waters. Like a mass of shimmering raindrops, they fall back quickly beneath the surface. The brief appearance has instantaneous effect. Some of the birds submerge instantly like submarines, while others dive swiftly and leave barely a ripple. One after another they reappear. Some still gulp while slender lumps are obvious in their thin, long throats. Others still carry fish in sharp-toothed jaws. With this first catch the feeding frenzy is on. Again and again the birds dive deep and long into the greenish depths. These extinct birds are masters of underwater swimming. With the swiftness and clean sliding shape of torpedoes, they pursue fish. Their feet are powerful and webbed. They are placed far back on the body to give a strong push underwater.

Suddenly a shadow passes overhead. In the sky, like a swiftly moving cloud broken into small particles, a flock of birds wheel and turn. These white pigeon-sized creatures with bluish gray heads are *Icthyornis*. They resemble modern terns. Searching for food, they flash above the waters briefly, then wheel and disappear around an outcropping of land.

The sun rises high in the sky. At midday it is hot. As though exhausted by fishing, one large flightless bird after another approaches the pebbly beach and jumps upward. It is difficult for these seal-sized creatures to move on land. Their watery grace and swiftness are gone. Awkwardly they push themselves forward on bellies to a comfortable spot. Now for a time they preen and rest. The calls are muted and gradually die away. There is no sound but the slap of waves and the distant calls of crickets. The ancient afternoon moves on.

The Cretaceous period stretched from 135,000,000 to 63,000,000 years ago. During it there were primitive flamingos and cormorantlike birds in addition to *Hesperornis* and *Icthyornis*. All these new avian forms were specialized and very different from the primitive structure of *Archaeopteryx*. There must have been many other birds that existed between the two periods. But we know nothing of them.

Continuing through time, you realize there are many more birds now extinct. Between 63,000,000 and 36,000,000 years ago a great number of avian forms developed until they outnumbered the reptiles. There were herons, ducks, hawks, owls, shorebirds, pelicans, ostriches. All were primitive, but their offspring have continued changing and developing to form the species we know today. There were also some huge flightless birds. *Diatryma* was as large as a horse. It had a huge, heavy bill and strong legs for running down and killing reptiles and mammals. We know these birds only as fossils.

There were so many ancient wings—and yet so few. Since 1861 only four other specimens of *Archaeopteryx* have been found. The last was uncovered in 1973. The bones of more recent birds are discovered in greater numbers but are still relatively few. We have good fossil records of many much earlier forms. It does not seem to make sense that so few specimens of *Archaeopteryx* and other birds have been found. Were there really so few of these birds, or is there some other reason?

We know that our record of avian evolution is very rough. One expert in fossil bird bones has estimated that a total of 1,634,000 species of birds live or have lived. That is about 1,624,600 more bird species than we know about today. The bones of birds are fragile and easily destroyed by fossilization. This is not as true of many other living things. Mollusks have hard shells. Mammals and large reptiles have solid bones and teeth. Such things are more easily preserved than the dainty hollow bones of birds. Another factor is that most birds seldom became stuck and died in mud or water, where their skeletons would easily have been preserved. Probably most lived and died over the dry lands. In the forests or in the open areas their bodies were eaten or bones scattered by other animals. Wind, rain, and heat also contributed to destroying them so that no traces were left. Maybe someday the rocks will give us more evidence. Of the forms and the life-styles of other ancient birds, we can only now guess.

Between 13,000,000 and 2,000,000 years ago some of our modern birds appeared. This also was a time of great variety and numbers of feathered creatures. Today some more recent groups of birds such as passerines, or perching birds, and the swifts and hummingbirds are increasing in species numbers, while many others are growing less. From very long ago until now birds continue evolving, changing, moving, and sometimes dying out. We cannot predict the direction of evolution. One can only think, wonder, watch, and try to understand a bit from the ancient wings of the past.

(Top) Blue Jay, (right) Cedar Waxwing, (left, from top to bottom) Yellow Throat, Black-throated Blue Warbler, Myrtle Warbler, Blackburnian Warbler

4

Living Airplanes

On a lake in Yellowstone National Park a trumpeter swan prepares to fly. This is not an easy business for a 20-pound bird. First he must gain speed. The brilliantly white body begins to move. Faster and faster across the cold northern lake the swan both paddles and flies. After many yards it rises from the water. Its feet splatter rapidly across the wind-riffled surface. At last, like an airplane rising from its runway, the swan curves its route and moves slowly upward.

As the lake falls below, the large bird gives its plaintive trumpeting call. The sound is deep and loud, like a French horn. The long wings extend outward to 95 inches and beat in a strong and steady fashion. The body becomes more streamlined. The neck is straight forward, the feet pressed backward against the tail and rump. At full speed the trumpeter swan can fly 40 miles per hour.

Near the tops of Western mountains and high above the patchwork farms and glittery cities of the East fly several species of a type of bird that seems born to spend its life flying. Swifts spend more time flying than any other airborne creature. Their wings are crescent-shaped and thin, their bodies smooth and bullet-shaped for moving quickly through the air. With rapid, shallow wingbeats and short, sharp glides these birds twist and rocket almost effortlessly: 25, 50, more than 100 miles per hour! The wingbeats are so rapid they become a blur.

High-speed photographs taken of swifts in flight show a remarkable fact. One wing sometimes moves faster than the other. There is a reason for this. The tails of swifts are short and do not make effective rudders. The different speed of wingbeats is one way they steer.

Trumpeter Swans

Many people believe swifts never land. Though seeming plausible, this is not true. Swifts never land on branches or on the ground. They have short legs and small, weak feet that will not support them in such places. Instead, they cling upright with sharp toenails to tree trunks, caves, cliffs, chimneys.

Throughout human history people have watched birds and wished to fly. How would it feel to escape the gravitational force that held one so tightly? What joy it must be to move light wings and spring gently into the air! In the end the dream became a reality. Humans learned to build airplanes by studying the flight of birds.

Only in the last century has this happened. For most of us the reality is far different from the ideas of the first dreamers. A few women and men may build their own aircraft or flying machines. They may still leap into an excitement of sky and ride wind currents or glide to some safe landing place. For the majority of people, however, flight is far from an individual or well-understood experience. We have large and carefully constructed machines that can carry hundreds of people.

22

Timetables, roaring jets, music, motion pictures, magazines, and dinner served hot 20,000 feet into the sky—all combine to make us forget we have attained the dream of the ages. We are human, wingless, heavy, and naked of feathers—yet like the birds, we fly.

The solid body of a large modern plane may seem to have little in common with a bird. Planes *are* far different from those feathered creatures with whom they share the air, but not to so great a degree as you might think. Birds and planes fly on the same principles and use much of the same equipment. Wings, propellers, and steering gear are used by both, as are slots and flaps and retractable equipment that help in takeoff and landing. Essentially, birds are living airplanes.

In order to understand flight, you must keep one big fact in mind. Air is a fluid. It has weight and pressure like any other and the push is in all directions: upward, downward, from each side.

A man named Daniel Bernoulli first studied how the pressure of a moving fluid changes with the speed of its motion. He found that when the flow is speeded up, the pressure decreases. You can easily test this yourself. Hold a sheet of paper, and blow across its upper surface. The bent portion of the paper will rise and begin to straighten out as you blow. This is because the air pressure against it is being reduced by the faster airspeed of your breath. The air below the paper now has the heavier push upward. This principle applies to flight.

Both the wing of a bird and the wing of an airplane are essentially objects inserted into a flow of air. If the shape of both top and bottom of the wing were the same, there would be no lift and no flight. Air would go the same distance at the same speed on both. If you take a piece of cardboard and bend it, you may more easily understand. Air hitting the upper curved surface follows the bend; that on the lower moves straight across. The curved distance is much greater.

Bird wings bulge upward to one degree or another, depending on the species. Airplane wings have copied this. The tops are rounded; the bottoms flattened. By Bernoulli's principle we would predict that the air crossing the wing top will move faster and have less pressure than the air moving below. This is exactly what happens. The difference between the pressures creates a push upward that is called lift.

The wings of birds are really two parts with very different functions. We can divide them into the inner part or arm which operates from the shoulder joint and the outer part or hand which is separated by a wrist midway along the wing. On the "thumb" of the hand is a group of feathers called the alula. These stick out from the wing. During slow flight they guide the air over the upper surface of the feather and prevent stalling. It is the arm that has the bent shape and supplies the lift. The outer half is the propelling or forward pushing part.

Bird wings have propellers. You might wonder why you haven't seen them. Are there hidden whirring blades you have not noticed before?

The answer is yes—to a degree. The propellers are there, bladelike and twisting. The speed is too fast for us to see them without help, however. A slowed-down motion picture of a bird taking flight would make obvious something you probably hadn't noticed before. With every downward stroke the air pushes against the front wing feathers, which are called primaries. They have the slightly curved blade shape of an airplane propeller. For a second or so with each stroke the primaries take on a twisted form and then recoil. These are the propellers of a bird and are the key to their forward-moving flight. When some birds reach the height desired, they spend time gliding with wings outstretched on the lift of the air. At these times the primaries usually lie flat. They increase the size of the wing and add to its lift in the air.

As the swan and the swift are very different in their patterns of flight and living, so are the wings different from each other for different birds. The gull is a glider. It has light, long, narrow wings. The primary feathers are attached only loosely. Such a design allows the feathers to move and respond easily to very slight wind shifts. Other birds that are strong, swift fliers have very tightly fitted primaries. This is true of the racing pigeon and the falcon. The structure creates a powerful propeller. There are many other variations: short wings and long wings, wide and thin wings. There are immense differences from bird to bird. Tails are used for steering and also differ in shape and size. No matter what the shape of wings or tail, the same aerodynamic principles apply.

Feathers, wings, and Bernoulli's principle do not alone create a living airplane. There are two additional outstanding requirements for flying machines. One is low weight.

With its wings outstretched a full seven feet, a frigate bird glides above the mirrored morning waters of southern Florida. Schools of silvery mullet leap into sunlight. The huge bird swoops gracefully upon them. Smoothly he captures several in the air, then glides lower to pluck a jellyfish or squid from the surface with his large curved

beak. In this way he often badgers gulls or other water birds until they throw up their food. None can outfly the frigate bird. His body seems as light as a kite floating smoothly on the air—and no wonder. There are only four ounces of bones in the huge body.

The bones of birds weigh very little. Many are thin, hollow, filled with air, yet are strong and elastic. In parts of the skeleton lightweight reinforcements are built in, like the struts of an airplane. Other bones are fused or blended together. The breastbone must form a firm support for the powerful wing muscles; the backbone no longer bends, as does the human's. In addition, some parts are missing and the center of gravity is shifted toward the middle of the bird. The long lizard tail has disappeared. Heavy, bony jaws with teeth have been replaced with strong but light horny beaks. Feathers are extremely strong and light: In these characteristics they outdo anything humans have created.

The second requirement for a flying machine is high power.

A bird in the hand is very hot. In small birds the body quivers, and the breathing is very fast. Without water and food these feathered

25

creatures rapidly die. For their weight birds eat more food, use more oxygen, and give off more heat than any other animal with a backbone.

Humans have body temperatures of only 98.6 degrees Fahrenheit. We would die if the thermometer registered 106 degrees. Such temperatures are normal for birds, however. The bodies of some thrushes hover at 110.5 degrees. The normal temperatures of all birds are above 105 degrees. There is a chemical law that says the speed of a reaction doubles with each 10 degrees Centigrade rise in temperature. This applies inside a body, as well as outside it. High body temperatures give birds speedy chemical reactions which are necessary for quick muscle contraction during flight.

There are problems, as well as advantages, to the body heat of birds. At high temperatures fuels burn rapidly. Birds must feed their internal furnaces often and with very high-energy foods. Seeds, fruits, worms, and insects usually are eaten. Few birds can afford to consume such bulky low-calorie things as leaves and grass. Additional specializations help birds with their high-energy needs. The digestive system is extremely efficient and quick. A cedar waxwing can eat berries and totally digest them in sixteen minutes. Other small perching birds may take only a half hour to two hours. Most parts of the foods are used. Very little nourishment is wasted.

Birds have a system of air sacs in addition to lungs. These extend all through the body and help remove the heat created by flying. In addition, a big rapidly beating four-chambered heart pushes blood quickly through the body. Tissues are given nourishment and oxygen; wastes are removed.

There are many specializations in birds. We have discussed only a few. Others include weight reduction by eggs laid outside the body and sex organs that don't develop except for the short time each year when they are needed. The eye has grown in importance, and the brain changed to allow for it. Birds almost have lost the sense of smell. There are many ways the body is uniquely fitted to life in the air and different from the bodies of those that mainly walk and crawl and swim.

Life in the air makes severe and special demands. It is like a knife whittling and paring away all unnecessary things and shaping additional traits that will aid. The design of nearly every bird is for flying. The structures both inside and out are solutions to the problems of flight. This is true of modern flightless birds, as well as those that fly. Both groups had aerial ancestors.

5

Early on a Spring Morning

In the last hours of springtime darkness, there comes an echoed, steady drumming. The rhythm is slow at first, then accelerates to a fluttering heartbeat sound. At last the pounding breaks. For a while there is silence; then the slow thumping begins again. The sound is a love call: an attracting signal for a mate. Somewhere in this pale-green woodland there is a male ruffed grouse. To make the sound, he perches on a hollow log and vigorously moves his cupped wings downward and forward, then back and upward in the air.

Darkness fades, but it is not yet dawn. *Chewink . . . chewink.* A towhee flies from branch to branch of an elm tree and continues his call. The sounds of the morning increase rapidly. Before the sun's light streams over the horizon the world is loud and raucous.

Chickadees, catbirds, cardinals, ovenbirds, towhees, juncos, and many others add to the din. A tufted titmouse gives a clear loud whistle: *Peeto . . . peeto . . . peeto.* The small gray body—restless as skittering raindrops—moves rapidly from branch to branch. A male robin gives a single bright call note, then moves scurry-stop-scurry-stop across the wet lawn. Brilliant yellow meadowlarks sing on fence posts. Far back in the woodland a thrush begins a clear flutelike song. A yellow-shafted flicker flips from one tree to another. As it does so it gives its ringing cry of *wick . . . wick . . . wick.* Then, with tail bracing it upright against a tree, it begins to drum with a loud and rapid beat. A house wren chitters while gathering dried grasses and string. With its mouth full, it continues to sing. This tiny bird seems a mass of violent activity. It flutters one way, then another; with ferocity and

(*Top left*) House Wren, (*center*) Cardinal, (*top right*) House Sparrow

ease it chases much larger birds. A hole in a pole, a clothespin bag, a small passage on the corner of the house—all these places it stuffs with materials. The wren may build as many as three or four nests before it settles on using only one.

There is a rhythm to bird sounds in these slowly lengthening spring days. The most vigorous singing begins at dawn or before. It softens, dampens, eases up to a low point in early afternoon. In the evening there is a new wave of singing, although it is not as loud or exuberant as in the morning. A few birds such as wrens and vireos sing with vigor the whole day, and others continue long into the dark.

All winter a few birds sang or called. The cardinal seemed a moving dash of blood against the snow. Occasionally he whistled his loud, clear, reedy song. Chickadees flittered nervously in the leafless branches and called a raspy *tsecka-dee-dee-dee*. In general, however, the air was muted as though all bird sounds were absorbed by the piling snow.

For the months of cold many bird species moved away. On the coasts

of Florida, California, or South America, on the Southern green river bottoms and red mud streams, there is more food. In these places the migrants have spent an easier time. The longer days trigger a change within them. The sex organs of both males and females begin to grow larger. Chemicals—called hormones—spill from these into the blood. With such changes a nervousness possesses the birds. In the night dark or the brightest day, in streams of the same species, mixed flocks or alone, they take to the air and pour steadily back toward summer breeding ranges.

In many places the spring change is slow. There is a bit more song. A few new birds move among the trees. Slowly the trickle thickens. In other places the spring clamor comes with sudden intensity that is short-lived. One morning the woodland seems relatively empty; on the next the pines, the dogwoods, the maples, and other trees glitter with small, sharp-billed, active birds. There are flashes of gold, orange, black, and olive green. There is a din of buzzing, low-pitched notes. This is the northward migration of warblers. The stream extends for

29

miles. In it there are many, many species; each has a different coloration and song. In a few days most of the birds will be gone.

Slow or fast, the spring change in birds carries the same internal command. It is spring! One must sing! One unmated song thrush spent ten hours singing, nine hours roosting, and five hours eating. A red-eyed vireo sang 22,977 songs in a single day.

Birds are masters of sound production. In no other animal group is this ability so highly perfected and widely used. There are exceptions, of course. Storks, pelicans, and some vultures have no voice. A silent bird is a rarity, however. There are a variety of nonvocal sounds. Birds drum, whistle, or thump the air with wings or tail, pound with bills, stomp, and puff. Such noises are used for the same purposes as songs and calls.

More than half of all living birds are songbirds. This means they belong to the passerine group. All bird vocalizations are not song; some are calls. A call is a brief relatively simple sound. A song is much longer. It is a series of different notes or a single note repeated in some sort of specific pattern. Usually only male birds sing, but the female cardinal and rose-breasted grosbeak can do so almost as well as the males. In general, passerines sing while other birds call. Though the killdeer and mourning dove are not passerines, they sing well.

Many people believe birds sing from joy, but this is far from the basic reason. Song is like all other activities in the lives of birds. It must help in the survival of the species.

In general, sounds of birds have three functions. The most important is reproductive. Songs, calls, and other noises advertise to perspective mates while warning others of the species of territorial boundaries. Bird sounds stimulate and synchronize courtship and mating behavior. Mates and young often are identified by calls. These, in turn, make the bond between family members stronger.

A second use of sound is as a signal between birds of a species. The proper call can bring a flock together to rally against a predator, keep individuals in touch in dense bushes and dark forest lands, or spread word of food or danger. Songs or calls may be used to scare away enemies.

A third function of the voice is very individual. Birds get rid of nervous energy by sound, or they spend time practicing their songs. It is not unusual to see a bird sitting alone and singing with a soft, hesitant voice. So it's possible that sometimes birds *do* sing for pleasure or joy. There is no way to know, for we cannot talk with birds.

1. Rose-breasted Grosbeak 2. Meadowlark 3. Robin 4. Catbird 5. Tufted Titmouse
6. Chickadee 7. Slate-colored Junco 8. Towhee

Not all birds have the same number of songs or calls. Domestic chickens have ten different calls; a domestic pigeon has only four. The male house wren gives three different songs for three different purposes: defending the territory, mating, and defense. Another passerine bird—the common house sparrow—has eleven notes. Each is used in the proper situation. Identification, love calls, male social song, flight signal, danger signal, call for fledged young, and nest relief are all part of the species vocabulary.

When we listen to birds or watch them sing, it seems very easy. For birds it is. They have the right mental and physical equipment, which we have not. We can raise our voices from low to high. Tremulous patterns or sudden shifts and turns are very difficult, however. Even our whistles are simple, rigid, and flat compared to those of most birds.

Birds do not have a larynx as humans do. Instead, they have a unique boxlike structure called a syrinx. It is located at the lower end of the trachea, or air pipe. Two pairs of elastic membranes stretch across the box. When air from the lungs is forced through them, it vibrates. The basic plan is similar to that of a woodwind instrument such as a clarinet and flute.

The trachea acts as an organ pipe. Its length, diameter, and rigidity all influence bird sound. Both the trumpeter swan and the whooping crane have enormously long windpipes which give a deep, trombone-like quality to their calls.

Muscles in the membranes and the rings of the syrinx walls change the pitch of the voice. Generally the more muscles, the greater variety in song and call. There are exceptions, however. Crows have seven pairs of muscles but are poor singers.

The song of birds is their natural heritage. A few species have a critical age during which they must learn the species song. If they do not hear it and are exposed to another instead, they will learn the wrong song. Even for those birds that have the proper song, there are variations that may help individuals recognize each other. Some birds duet—each warbling a part of a shared melody. This also may aid in individual recognition.

For many birds the complex trills—the complicated patterns—are not learned. The knowledge of how and what to sing is transmitted in the genes or inherited material of each species. As with nest building and flight, many such birds grow more skilled with practice. Beyond this they need not learn.

6

Dawn Dance

Some of the land of the West is called high desert. There is snow in the winter and small amounts of rain at other times. Altogether it does not add up to more than 10 inches per year. Upon the low, rolling hills and wide troughs of valleys there are hardy plants that can live with little water. Sage and rabbit brush grow easily. In the lower places there is more moisture. Here sagebrush grows taller than a man and a foot thick at the base. Bright yellow lichens cover the rocks. In the spring there are many small, low-growing plants.

On a patch of desert far from any city there is a flattened open area about 200 yards wide and one half mile long. Here the roots of plants have not yet dug in. The ancient lava flow is hard. A few potholes glitter with water. This is a lek, or booming ground or strutting ground. It is the courtship place of sage grouse. Each year as many as 400 of these chicken-sized birds return to the same area to display and to breed. Some travel as far as 50 to 100 miles. This lek is smaller than some and larger than others. A display ground may be 1 to 40 acres in size.

It is late February when the males arrive. The snows barely have left. Hens are not yet present. Morning and evening the cocks congregate on the lek and begin to strut and display. Males face males with hostility. They fight, threaten, and bluff to establish their positions. Sage grouse society is not at all democratic. These few weeks are very important. They will determine which birds gain the central part of the lek and which will be forced to remain on the fringes.

When two cocks prepare to fight, they stand side by side, head to tail, about 15 to 18 inches apart. The body, wings, and tail quiver.

Each bird begins a rapid and repetitious guttural challenge. Suddenly the wing of one lashes out. It is aimed at the head of the other bird. Its rival may first parry—or strike back immediately. A number of blows are exchanged. At last one bird slowly backs away. The winner does not follow. Instead, he begins to strut.

There is one very important patch of land. The bird that gains its ownership is called the supercock. He will do almost all the mating. Near him is the subcock, his closest rival. If the supercock were killed, the subcock would take over the breeding. With luck, near the end of the season, he may mate with a few hens. Most of the male grouse on the grounds will not mate at all.

The supercock is not always the largest bird, but he is always the most vigorous, active, and ready to fight. A lot of this behavior probably is determined by the amount of hormones in his blood and his general health. It is these sage grouse strengths that he passes on to his offspring. The species remains healthy and strong.

Once some scientists experimented to see what would happen if both the supercock and the subcock were gone. Twice they removed the dominant birds from the very similar breeding world of prairie chickens. The normally orderly society fell apart. Males spent so much time fighting that they seldom mated. There were not many fertile nests that year.

At last the sage grouse females arrive. In the dimness of early dawn, in the white softness of full moonlit nights, they walk among the displaying cocks. Although they are smaller than the males, they resemble the males in many ways. Both sexes have narrow, pointed tails and feathering to the base of the toes. Backs and sides are a mixed pattern of grayish brown, buff and black. Females have almost no white on the chest, while males have a great deal. This is to the female's benefit. She must not look too much like a cock, or she will be attacked.

With bodies low and feathers slicked, the hens move across the breeding grounds. Nearby cocks strut with greater frequency. A male sage grouse is particularly adapted to attract the attention of a mate. As the birds move forward in mincing steps, they swallow more air for each of four big gulps. Large hanging white ruffs called esophageal pouches balloon out. On the last puff, patches of bare mustard-green skin bulge outward in the white. The head almost disappears into the enormous ruff. Then all the air is released from the pouches. The ruff falls with a *plop-plop* sound that may be heard a half mile away on a quiet morning. During the display the male also moves his wings back

and forth. They brush against the sides of his breast and the stiff white feathers on his neck with a resonant, squeaking, swishing sound.

At first the females seem barely aware what is going on. They peck at the ground and roam about the lek nonchalantly. As the season continues, more and more are ready to mate. They begin to gather in groups of fifty to seventy in a breeding area near the supercock. One female after another steps into his territory and squats with wings outstretched. This is an invitation to mate. A male may fertilize as many as fifteen to twenty hens in a morning.

After breeding, a female runs a few steps, then ruffles her feathers. She does not remain nearby for long. With rapid wingbeats and a quick horizontal flight she disappears. Hens may travel many miles before making a nest.

Most mating is over before the dawn. With noisy wings the sage grouse fly away. The early sunlight falls upon an empty lek. In a place so exposed, dawn courtship is the safer way. Here golden eagles live. In the daylight they move silently across the sky. There are nighttime predators, too, but the danger to breeding birds is not so great. Hunting cries echo in the night. Each year some of the birds are killed by packs of coyotes that roam the hills. To the sage grouse as a species, this does not matter greatly. The outlying males are vulnerable. The supercock is safe inside, as are the hens that wait near his territory. Nature has selected well. Sage grouse life goes on.

The rigid and elaborate ritual of the sage grouse strutting is only one form of bird courtship. Males and females attract each other in many ways. Wattles, crowns, colorful feet, and brilliantly marked mouth cavities appeal to mates. Songs, flights, noises, and bright body coloration function the same way. Voiceless storks clap mandibles together. Some pigeons and owls clap the wings over the back. Other birds spar with bills, "kiss," caress, entwine necks, and nibble at each other's feathers.

Snipes have elaborate courtship flights. The male circles high in the air, then zooms downward over the female. As the air rushes through his narrow wing and tail feathers, there is a loud buzzing sound. The closely related woodcock sings during its courtship flight. In the late afternoon or early evening or on damp and foggy nights it circles high into the air and whistles a beautiful series of trills. The female sits on the ground. She waits passively for him to flutter down.

Bitterns attract their mates with special loud calls. They belch, bray, and make deep, gulping noises. The sounds are not loud yet carry for long distances.

Great blue herons "dance" with courtship. In early April these large birds group together on mud banks or sandbars and begin to circle. They extend and flap their wings. The males flash bills at one another. The females dance but do not fight. Instead, they give loud, croaking cries. After a time the birds pair off and nest. Peace returns.

The closely related American egret has a less strenuous form of courtship. On sandbars or cleared areas the males strut back and forth and display their plumes. They give deep-throated calls.

36

Male mourning doves strut around females. Their heads bob back and forth; the tails are flaired. Occasionally male and female rub bills and coo softly.

Courtship does three major things. Where both sexes are externally similar, it divides males from females. Mating, nest building, and egg development all are stimulated by such shared displays. For birds that nest and raise the young together, courtship strengthens the attachment, or pair bond. Some birds pair for life, some for a year or a single brood of young. Others—like the sage grouse—mate for only a few seconds.

Usually only males have bright colors and elaborate behaviors to attract a mate. Where male and female look very much alike, usually both take approximately equal parts in the courtship. In a few cases the usual roles are completely reversed. The female phalarope—a shorebird—is larger and brighter in its mating plumage than the male. It is also the first to arrive on the breeding grounds and takes the more active part in the courtship. After laying eggs, the female leaves. The male incubates the eggs and cares for the young.

These are only a few of the varieties of bird courtship. The list could go on and on. Some are elaborate, graceful, and beautiful to human eyes; others seem grotesque and ungainly. In either case, the rituals work very well for the birds that use them and allow the survival of the species.

(Center) Sandhill Cranes, (top right) Sandhill Cranes in courtship dance, (bottom right) Whooping Crane

TYPES OF NESTS 1. Shearwater 2. Fairy Tern 3. King Penguin 4. Oriental Swiftlet
5. Swallow 6. Killdeer 7. Megapode

7

A Work of Weaving

Winter. In the low, intertwined growth of wild cherry or willow, in the tops of poplars or elms, or in the protected forks of apple trees deserted bird's nests suddenly are visible. There are solid mud-lined cups and flexible swinging bags, tiny woven cradles, and massive jumbles of twigs and bark.

The variety can be amazing. The nests familiar to most people are the neat cup-shaped variety made by the songbirds, or passerines. Most other orders of birds build simple affairs which at best seem little more than an elevated platform of twigs. Herons, crows, and magpies make unruly stick-tangled nests. After one brood they rebuild. Hawks, kites, falcons, and owls often take over such deserted creations. Shearwaters hatch their eggs in old rabbit burrows near the sea. The fairy tern lays one egg on the bare branch of a tree. Slight scrapped depressions on the flats where they live form the nests of killdeer. Their eggs match the background perfectly.

Swallows dig holes into banks by water or plaster beehivelike creations to the undersides of bridges or rocky cliffs. The nests of king and emperor penguins are the birds themselves. These flightless Antarctic creatures simply hold an egg on the top of their webbed feet. A patch of bare belly skin folds over and keeps it warm. Perhaps the most unusual nest belongs to the megapods, or mound builders. A pair of these Australian or Malayan fowl rakes a mound of litter and dirt five to seven feet high. In it the female digs a hole and lays a single egg. She need never incubate it. The heat from the decaying plant materials does that job.

Where birds build their nests may be as important as the style. Robins often choose sites close to people. The same is true of pigeons, starlings, sparrows, and wrens. There are problems and dangers to such habits, but the benefits are greater. Most hawks would not dare come so close to human habitation. Snakes are rare. Of the many creatures that might prey on young, eggs and adults in wilder places, cats alone remain.

Humans are not the only animals used by nesting birds in this way. Some relatively helpless birds weave a nest very close to those of larger, more aggressive species. Sparrows, grackles, and other small birds build on the edges or undersides of nests of storks, owls, ospreys, hawks, or eagles. For some reason they are seldom bothered by their large, protective hosts.

To house our young and ourselves, we build elaborate heavy structures that we live in year after year. It is hard to imagine going to such great amounts of work and then deserting our homes again and again. Yet that is what most birds do. There is good reason. An old nest may be weakened by storm and wind and use. It might break with the weight of new eggs or young. A whole brood would be lost. In addition, old nests often are hiding places for tiny mites and other parasites that feed on and weaken the young. A few birds continue to use the same nest, however. Storks and eagles may simply add new materials to the mass each season for ten or more years. Huge nests are the result. That of a European white stork was found to weigh more than a ton. A bald eagle in Florida had a nest about 18 feet deep and 9 feet wide.

Nest building usually is hard work. It takes the average songbird about 280 trips to make a simple cup nest. The availability of materials, how far they must be carried, the time of the year, the weather, and how the labor is shared—all determine exactly how much work each bird must do. It is hard to predict the labor, however. Robins sometimes become confused by good fortune. Faced with plenty of materials and lots of good building sites they flutter frantically from place to place. One, two, three, or four different nests may be built. The female may lay eggs in several before she incubates one.

The building of a nest may be done only by the female. Hummingbirds and red-eyed vireos follow this pattern. Kingfishers, woodpeckers, and swallows are a few of the many birds that share about equally in the yearly labor. Female doves and pigeons build the nest alone, but the male brings the materials. Some shrikes and a few other male

40

FEMALE NEST BUILDERS 1. Ruby Throat **2.** Baltimore Oriole **3.** Mexican Cowbird **4.** Robin **5.** House Martin

birds build the nest completely unaided by their mate. The male frigate bird builds the nest, but the female brings him materials.

What are nests made of? The answer sounds a bit like the old refrain "snips and snails and puppy dog tails." Many different materials are used. The most common are grasses, leaves, mosses, twigs, dung, pebbles, flowers, wood, hair, feathers, snake skins, bones, spider webs, beetle wings, stones, mud, sand, and mussel shells. The oriental swift makes its nest entirely from its own saliva.

The male northern oriole is probably one of the most brightly colored birds in North America. Its clear, loud call carries far in the springtime woods. Less obvious is the female bird. Her yellowish olive or brown feathers blend easily against the foliage and make her hard to see. She is outstanding in her own way, however. This rather drab passerine bird is considered by many the greatest artist of nest building.

For the female oriole, as for other birds, nest building is an instinctive activity. At birth the pattern already is in her brain. It takes only the trigger. Older birds sometimes make better nests, but even first-season builders need no lessons.

Early in the year the female oriole begins her work. The trees are leafless. The winds are cold. These things do not slow her activity. About 30 feet high in an elm tree she selects a flexible limb. With grapevine bark, Indian hemp, grass, string, horsehair, or cloth she starts her weaving. The first long strands wind loosely about the branch; later threads draw these more tightly together. Gradually a loose snarl of fibrous material is formed.

The male oriole sings, catches insects, and sometimes brings nesting materials. The female pays him little attention. She works steadily and without hesitation. The movements of her bill are shuttlelike and often too rapid to count. One hundred thrusts at each visit are not unusual. Each new thread must be woven into the nest.

After two to three days of work the nest is still a loose tangled mass of fibers. There are many long, dangling strands. Now the female oriole works from the inside. She places one foot on the twig, the other on the nest material. With spread wings she balances herself. Above, below, or to either side she thrusts and probes. Each movement brings in new strands or gathers up old. When the five- to six-inch-deep pocket is complete, she lines it with softer materials such as hair, wool, fine grasses, or milkweed down. To shape the cup, she settles down and

42

shakes all over. Again and again she turns and repeats the movement.

The nest building takes from five to fifteen days. The finished product is a dangling woven bag with an entrance on the side or top. It is almost impossible for any without wings to reach it. In such a swaying, well-made cradle the eggs will be safe. Even humans have a hard time finding such nests. In later spring or summer it will be hard to see. The grayish color blends well with the silvery leaf undersides of the elm.

8
The Enormous Effort

Fish may lay millions of eggs per year. A half-inch-long mayfly spews out 200 to 500 eggs. Frogs extrude large gelatinous masses that will develop into many tadpoles. Compared to these animals, the reproduction of birds may appear very inefficient.

This is far from true, however. The total number of eggs is not as important as the number of babies that survive. Fish, frogs, and may-flies do not care for their young. Eggs and the newly hatched individuals develop alone. A billion dangers are hidden in their watery nurseries. Of the hundreds of millions of young and eggs only two need survive to replace the parents in a stable population. The rest hold up the pyramid of life in a different way. Animals must eat living food. The surplus fish, frogs, and insects feed other hungry things that grow.

Birds produce only a small number of eggs. These they guard and incubate very carefully. The young hatch at a growth stage closer to adulthood than do the young of frogs or insects. The babies are protected and given large amounts of care.

In some ways a bird egg is an infant of the species plus a package of liquid food. Reptiles, birds, and a few primitive mammals are the only vertebrates that have their embryos outside both the body and the water. The heavy shell is necessary; it resists drying and protects developing young. It creates new problems also. Urea is the most common waste product of animals. It is highly poisonous and easily dissolved in fluid. In the water or in the bodies of females there is no large problem. Easily and quickly the poisons flow away from the developing young. For embryos developing in a shell, urea would be lethal, however.

Birds and reptiles have solved the problem in the same way. They

(*Top left*) Black Skimmers, (*bottom right*) Canada Goose

produce uric acid rather than urea. This white crystalline substance will not dissolve and harm the delicate developing tissues. Harmlessly it is stored within the shell. Uric acid gives an additonal bonus to birds. The white pasty waste is lighter than the watery urine of mammals. It reduces the load for flying creatures.

For birds, egg laying is a very "expensive" activity. The physical act of extruding these large oval objects requires a large amount of energy. A female Canada goose, for example, takes about four hours to lay an egg. During this time the female raises the front end of her body, opens her mouth, and breathes rapidly. Her wings spread and vibrate. They drop to the sides of the nest. Finally she opens her beak widely and seems to be straining hard. When she relaxes again, an egg has been laid.

Normally the Canada goose will lay four to ten eggs at intervals. She is an *indeterminate* layer, however. If her eggs are stolen, she will continue to lay until the "right" number is in the nest. Penguins, ducks, the chickenlike birds, woodpeckers, and some passerines also are indeterminate layers. One yellow-shafted flicker laid seventy-one eggs in seventy-three days when an experimenter continued to remove all but one. Geese and other birds probably do not count the eggs. The proper number or clutch size simply feels right. This information goes to the brain and glands. The egg formation process stops.

All the materials that make eggs must come from the body. For this reason many large temporary changes occur in female birds in the spring. Their digestive system becomes more efficient. Calcium for eggshells is one of the bigger needs. More foods containing calcium are eaten, and a larger portion than usual is absorbed by the body. Blood calcium may double. About 70 percent of that required comes from eating; the remaining 30 percent is removed from the long bones in the body. Blood contains more sugar and fat. Both give extra energy.

Eggs are created assembly-line fashion. The yolk and the ovum are released together and travel to the oviduct, where fertilization may occur. This part of the process takes an average of eighteen minutes. The developing egg remains about three more hours in the oviduct. A layer of the clear whitish albumen and a shell membrane are secreted about the tiny beginning. In the wider cup of the uterus, the egg may remain as long as twenty hours while the shell and coloration are added. Muscles in the uterus wall determine its final shape. At last the egg is laid.

Eggs come in many shapes, sizes, colors, and finishes. Most are smooth and dull, but those of storks are deeply pitted. The eggs of grebes and flamingos are rough on the surface. Woodpeckers have glossy eggs. The surface of many duck eggs is greasy and water-repellent. The eggs of hawks and eagles often have shortened oval shapes; those of owls and kingfishers are roundish. Long, elliptical eggs are laid by streamlined, rapidly flying birds such as swifts, hummingbirds, and swallows. Eggs of young that hatch as fairly capable chicks contain more yolk. They are proportionally bigger than the eggs of helpless young

The size, shape, surface, and color of eggs affect survival. Guillemots lay eggs very pointed at one end and broad at the other. These birds nest on the edges of rock ledges. The eggs do not roll. Shorebirds generally have pointy eggs and incubate them with the sharp ends in. The eggs fit more compactly. Heating and covering are easier and more efficient.

9
Stranger in the Nest

Both the common and scientific names of the brown-headed cowbird describe parts of its behavior well. The Indians called it buffalo bird. Now this black and brown bird feeds fearlessly about the heads and legs of domestic cattle. The scientific name, *Molothrus,* means vagabond, tramp, or parasite. The four to five finely spotted eggs are laid in the nests of other birds. Tyrant flycatchers, finches, vireos, and warblers are the four families usually parasitized. Song sparrows are the most common victim.

There are good reasons for the choice of host birds. Young cowbirds would not live on fish in a kingfisher's nest. The diet of a crow would be almost as strange. Young quail leave the nest at hatching and find their own food. Foster parents must live in a way similar to the cowbird, or the young will not survive. Not all birds that could serve as a host do so, however. Robins and catbirds throw strange eggs from the nest. The yellow warbler buries a strange egg in the bottom of the nest or builds a second story over the top. If a cowbird continues to lay, the warbler continues to build. The nest towers with two, three, four, or even five stories before the small yellow female begins to incubate her own eggs.

Usually the parasitized birds will accept any egg into the nest, although they may throw out anything that doesn't "feel right," such as punctured or cracked eggs. Sometimes feel doesn't seem to matter, however. Birds have incubated light bulbs, golf balls, watches, dice, and many other strange things. A few birds prefer anything bigger than usual. Geese will set upon ostrich eggs or larger artificial models while ignoring their own normal-sized creations.

(*Top right*) Yellow Warbler, (*bottom left*) Kirtland's Warbler

A lot of people feel a kinship with parasitized birds. They are enraged and disgusted by the cowbird's nonmotherly ways. These small brown creatures are called degenerate and promiscuous. Their eggs are thrown away.

It's easy to put human feelings into animals. Doing so is a loss, however. It is harder to see some of the fascinating things that really are happening. Very occasionally cowbirds do a large damage to their hosts. In Michigan Kirtland's warbler is in danger of becoming extinct. Nest parasitism is part of the problem. In general, however, cowbirds do little harm. They benefit farmers. In big flocks they feed and destroy large numbers of insects that might injure crops.

There is one very large rule of nature. For a species to survive, it must reproduce in some way. Cowbirds simply have developed a technique that is a bit different from that of most others. Probably at one time cowbirds built nests and raised their own young. There are relatives in South America that are only partly parasitic. The bay-winged cowbird uses the nests of other birds, but it lays all its eggs in the same place, incubates them, and raises its own young. The shiny cowbird is a very poor parasite. It lays many eggs where they will not hatch. Sometimes this bird tries unsuccessfully to build nests.

No one knows for sure how the parasitic habit began. There are several theories. Maybe the habit of following roaming herds made it impossible for cowbirds to raise their own young. Maybe somehow the natural rhythm of bird life became confused. Egg laying and nest building no longer fitted together in time. Eggs needed to be laid before a nest was ready.

No matter how brood parasitism began, it is a fascinating thing. If you watch carefully in spring, you may see a larger egg or a huge baby beside its smaller nest mates.

For several days a female song sparrow has been building her nest. Into a rose hedge she flutters again and again with beakfuls of grass. A female cowbird that has paired and mated carefully watches from a distance. If she approached too closely, both the male and female sparrow would attack. Watching the nest building stimulates her body. Her eggs begin to develop.

At last the nest is finished and the song sparrow lays her first egg. A little later the female cowbird flies to the ground nearby. As she runs or walks toward the nest, she seems unusually alert and nervous. At last she reaches the cup and jumps onto its edge. Her head swivels nervously. The song sparrows seem nowhere nearby. One minute passes, then two and three. At last the cowbird settles herself into the cup. In a few seconds the egg is laid.

Quickly the cowbird pierces one of the sparrow eggs with her beak. This egg she carries away and eats. Insects are the normal food of the cowbird. Only after laying does she steal an egg. Unless there is a shortage of nests, she will not lay in the same one twice. This does not guarantee the song sparrow will raise only one foster baby. There are other females looking for nests. Song sparrows sometimes incubate three or four cowbird eggs and none of their own.

When the adult song sparrow returns to the nest, she seems unaware of any change. At one-day intervals she continues laying her eggs, but she does not truly incubate them. Feathers keep warmth from reaching the eggs. Shortly before the fourth egg is laid, feathers fall from her breast and a bare area appears to form a brood pouch. It is spongy, hot, and richly supplied with blood. New blood vessels intrude into it until the whole area looks red and enflamed. Only now does incubation begin.

Incubation roughly equals pregnancy in mammals. In both cases the embryo is given warmth, protection, and food while it grows. There are advantages and disadvantages to eggs' developing outside the body. Both parents may share the work. If one partner is killed, the second may continue incubation. Sharing nest duties strengthens the pair bond between the adults. It encourages future feeding and care of the babies. On the other hand, it is fairly easy to desert eggs. Female mammals have no such choice.

The incubating song sparrow becomes quieter as time passes. At the beginning she spends about 60 to 80 percent of her time sitting on the nest. During bad weather she may remain even longer. Occasionally she raises up and turns the eggs. The heat from her body must be evenly distributed. Constant turning also keeps the egg membranes from sticking to the shell.

The male song sparrow does not incubate eggs. Instead he remains nearby. His territorial notes sound often. If another of his species enters the area, he will chase it away. Sometimes his mate joins him. Snakes, cats, dogs, and sometimes even people are attacked by both birds.

At times the female leaves the nest to feed. Her mate may follow her or may stay by the nest to protect it. She need not rush in her food finding. Even in cold weather there is no great hurry to return. The eggs of most birds can stand a great deal of chilling and still develop well. The major effect is in the time of incubation. Within limits, the warmer an egg remains, the shorter is the period to hatching.

Cowbird eggs have a shorter incubation period than that of most passerine birds. The foster baby appears first. It has a head start in both age and size. A day later the young song sparrows break from their shells. Both cowbird and song sparrows are naked, blind, and weak. Such baby birds are called altricial.

Helpless, or altricial, baby birds have special equipment and behavior that ensure they are fed. Immediately after the hatching the heads can wobble up, the beaks open. The light-colored hinge edges of

Song sparrow feeding young cowbird hatched in her nest. (*Bottom*) Brown-headed female cowbird.

the bill are called flanges. These areas contain many sensitive nerve endings. When the flanges are touched, the bill springs open. A brilliant yellow, red, or orange mouth cavity appears. Adult birds react instinctively to the bright coloration. Quickly they stuff the cavity full with insects or other food. With its big attractive mouth and large size, the baby cowbird gains more than its fair share of food.

The opening of the mouth is called gaping. At the beginning only a touch on the flanges causes it. Later the babies gape for many reasons. The enormous mouths fly open when the nest shakes, when the parent appears, or for the internal bite of hunger. The babies also develop cries which encourage adults to bring more food. Work for the parents is greater than if they raised only their own young.

With the hatching of the eggs, both male and female immediately

51

begin an exhausting and constant work. They must find lots of food of a very special type. Babies need high-protein diets in order to grow.

While the babies are tiny, the song sparrow parents bring food to the nest about five times an hour. When the young reach middle size, male and female average fifteen feedings per hour. During the last three days in the nest the babies clamor constantly. With wings sometimes drooping and much thinner than normal, the parents continue the work at an increased rate. They often make more than twenty-five visits to the nest every hour. Baby birds use their food well, however. They grow faster than any other backboned animal. Before they leave the nest, some young may increase fifty times the original weight and be larger than the adults.

Feeding is not the only task of parent birds. Newly hatched young must be incubated a lot. They cannot yet control their temperatures. This ability develops gradually. In the early stages, too, much chilling would be fatal. Babies must also be protected from wind, rain, hail and predators.

Keeping the nest clean is another job for the song sparrow parents. The feces of newly hatched nestlings are enclosed in a tough mucous membrane. These sacs usually are expelled immediately after the babies eat. Not all the food given to the young has been digested. Fats and proteins remain. For the first few days the parents consume the feces. While they are so busy, the wastes are a bonus of food energy. Later the sacs are carried away from the nest area and dropped. Feces immediately below a nest would be a dangerous marker; predators easily could find the young.

At last both song sparrows and cowbirds are fully feathered. All are ready to leave the nest. Suddenly the parents bring less food. No one knows why their behavior changes. Maybe instinctively they try to force the babies to leave the nest; possibly they simply are exhausted. The hunger of the babies increases. They become restless. One after another deserts the hidden cup. Parenthood is not over yet, however. For another ten to twelve days the male continues to feed the babies. With loud cries and gaping mouths they race after him. The cowbird is enormous compared to his nest mates. He is much larger than the adult song sparrow that continues to feed him.

The female has started another nest. She is setting on new eggs before the male at last drives away the almost fully grown young. The cowbird baby seems suddenly to recognize his true background. He deserts the song sparrows and joins the large flocks of feeding cowbirds.

10
Milk for Babies

Pigeons have been domesticated for centuries. They have been used for food and as messenger carriers, and today many people raise pigeons for fun or sport. There are racing pigeons, puffers, tumblers, and many other special breeds. Two hundred varieties now exist. Some have been bred for such a specialized appearance that they no longer can fly.

Pigeons belong to the order Columbiformes. Once there were three living families. The dodos and the solitairies are now extinct. These large flightless birds roamed the islands of the Indian Ocean until as late as 1800. Domestic pigeons and doves belong to the only surviving family. The mourning dove is probably the most common wild relative of the domestic pigeon. It is the only bird known to nest in all the land-connected forty-eight states in the United States.

Columbiformes have two very interesting abilities in common. All other birds drink by taking water in the mouth, then raising the head to allow liquid to run down the throat. Such a technique is slow. Doves and pigeons drink more quickly by suction. This unusual bird trait probably is related to a second special ability. All doves and pigeons make milk for their babies.

It is January. Snow swirls heavily from the mountains. The day grows dark at an early hour. Occasionally temperatures fall to twenty below. Inside a shed dusty with the whirring of many wings, a lone light bulb burns. Day and night it provides a strong yellowish glow and causes a great change in the lives of the domestic pigeons that live there. Temperature, snow, outside darkness are ignored. The twenty-

EXTINCT PIGEONS (*Left*) The Dodo, (*right*) Solitaires

four-hour light or long spring days cause the same general changes. The normally small reproductive organs grow; sex hormones flow in the bloodstream.

In midwinter these dark-gray birds are involved with mating. The males puff out iridescent throats. They move in strange bowing, jerky circles about the females. A rhythmical cooing fills the air. Gradually pairing takes place. Mating follows. The nests seem almost accidental: a slight hollow among a heap of boards, a place barely scrapped into dried dung, a few twigs gathered loosely together on the counter of a forgotten sink.

At last a female lays two small white eggs. For sixteen to eighteen days they must be incubated. Both birds take turns sitting on the nest. The male usually broods in the middle of the day, the female at other times. It is hard to tell the birds apart, for male and female pigeons are identical in appearance except for size: the male is larger.

The young pigeons hatch blind, helpless, and appearing naked be-

54

(Top left) Mourning Dove, *(center)* Stock Dove, *(right)* Rock Pigeon

neath their short white down. The skin is yellowish; the wobbly weak head has a large beak knob, or cere.

For the first week baby pigeons are fed milk that is very similar to that of rabbits. In both pigeons and rabbits fatty cells are shed from tissues. In the pigeon these come from special glands and the crop, forming a semifluid liquid that resembles cottage cheese.

The baby pigeons, or squabs, often start the feeding. A small bird crawls from beneath its parent, raises its head, and soundlessly begs for food. The adult immediately opens its mouth. Into this cavity the squab pushes its beak. The larger bill closes over. For a short while nothing seems to happen. Then the adult head begins a slow pumping motion; throat muscles violently twitch and contract. A minute passes before the adult bird opens her mouth. The baby sinks back beneath her.

The babies grow quickly on the plentiful and nutritious diet. The tough, resilient contour or veined feathers soon appear. At the beginning they are covered with a protective sheath. The baby is prickly with what are often called pinfeathers.

Feathers grow from the base next to the body, where the quill is alive. The inner core is pulpy and supplied with blood. Cells surrounding it form rapidly. With extreme speed they divide and push out. The base of the feather sinks deeply into the bird's skin. Age, diet, health are among the influences on the growth of feathers. The speed of this process may be different from feather to feather and bird to bird. When the feather is full-grown, it dies. The nourishing pulp disappears; the once growing cells become horny.

With the full sleek plumage the young pigeon looks very much like the adults. Male and female take their places in the social world of the coop.

When the common domestic pigeon lives in the wild, it is called a rock dove. In the country the adults feed on weed seeds and spilled grain. In the city rock doves have learned to rely a good bit on people. Pairs nest in old houses or the corners of buildings. Many city dwellers love them and feed them stale bread, peanuts, and other scraps; bags of such things are stored up. Children seem to dance as they race only inches behind these glistening waddling birds.

Pigeons are not welcomed by all, however. Many city officials consider rock doves a health hazard and a nuisance. In New York City alone there are about 5,000,000 of these wild birds, whose droppings stain buildings and streets. The dried feces may release organisms that can cause severe illness in humans.

56

11

Born to Swim

The young of song sparrows, cowbirds, pigeons, and many other birds are hatched helpless. Others are much more capable. The young of grebes, as well as those of ducks, geese, swans, chickens, and many others, are able to move around and find food almost immediately. These babies are fuzzy with heat-conserving down. Such young are called precocial. In a sense they spend their nestling stage within the egg.

Grebes look a bit like ducks and a bit like loons, yet they are neither. These small, sleek birds have long thin necks and slender, pointed bills. Their scientific name—Podicipediformes—means rump foots. It describes very well a peculiar aspect of the little bird's anatomy. The legs of grebes are set far back on the body. It's great for swimming but makes the bird almost helpless on land. Grebes do not do well in the air either. They are weak fliers that have difficulty taking off from the water.

Ponds and lakes form the natural home of grebes. Often it is difficult to see these aquatic birds, for they hide among reeds and dive swiftly through water after fish.

Grebes have a strange habit: Both male and female swallow their own feathers. Wads are found even in the stomachs of chicks a few days old. Feathers have no nutritional value. Possibly they simply trap and hold sharp fish bones until the digestive juices have softened them. Such pliable bones pass easily through the rest of the digestive tract without causing damage.

The nest of a grebe is a gently rocking cradle. Both male and female gather water plants into a floating platform anchored to a growing

1. Great Crested Grebe 2. Red-necked Grebe 3. Horned Grebe 4. Little Grebe 5. Pied-billed Grebe

(*Top*) Courtship dance ceremony of the Great Crested Grebe, (*bottom left*) female Great Crested Grebe with chicks, (*bottom right*) male offering fish to the female

plant. The nest is damp. To the human observer it may seem a poor place to hatch young, but the reverse is true. For many water birds such a moist nest is necessary. Those that nest too far away from water may have eggs that dry out. The developing young become desiccated. They die before hatching.

The female begins to incubate each egg as it appears. Most birds with precocial eggs wait until the last has been laid. There is good reason for waiting. Moving newly hatched young easily might be seen on land. Foxes, coyotes, and hawks quickly could wipe out a whole brood of young. The babies are led almost immediately to water. Staggered-aged nestlings could not survive. Those hatched a day or two later would be deserted.

In the floating cradle grebes' lives are more protected, however. During incubation male and female take turns on the nest. Occasionally, when both leave, they cover the three to ten eggs with rotting wet vegetation that keeps them warm and hides them.

Baby grebes are hatched to swim. After a short period of drying, each small chick pops into the water. Like fuzzy, whirling beetles, they move about looking for food. Their lobed toes begin to push and steer in the water. Such feet do not propel a grebe as quickly as the webbed feet of ducks, but they give a better control. Occasionally newly hatched grebes try to dive. But in their fuzzy down are many bubbles of trapped air which act like a life preserver that pops them back to the surface. Deep underwater swimming and the swift pursuit of fish are not yet for them. Many dangers lurk in the water; snapping turtles, large fish, and otters all eat young grebes.

The female continues to incubate her eggs, and the male stays close to his brood of precocial young. Suddenly there is a shadow. An eagle glides above the lake. Quickly the father gathers the young. Instinct tells the babies to clamber onto his back and hide beneath his head and wing feathers. Only their heads stick out.

Now the male grebe, expelling air from his air sacs and feathers, begins to sink deeper into the water. Silently and with hardly a ripple he moves. Only his head extends from the water like a periscope. At last he disappears completely. Not until he has reached the safety of the water plants do his head and body reappear. The young are no worse for the underwater jaunt. Diving is the grebe's major form of escape. Had he been surprised more suddenly, he would not have sunk slowly. With a quick flip he would have dived from the surface.

12
Finding the Way

Each spring and summer white pelicans nest in a colony on an island in the Great Salt Lake of Utah. There the naked, blind, helpless, and livid-skinned young are hatched. The parents take turns feeding and incubating them. As they gradually turn to fleecy, down-covered, then fully feathered young, baby pelicans need a lot of food. Each baby eats about 150 pounds of fish before it is able to fly.

No fish live in the Great Salt Lake. Adult pelicans may fly 30 to 100 miles a day to freshwater lakes. Despite the distance that must be traveled, food is easy to obtain. This is part of the reason for spring migration. Birds are spread out when their food needs are the greatest. There are many fertile lakes in the area and few fish eaters to compete for food.

This would not have been so if all the white pelicans had stayed on the wintering grounds. There would have been a great concentration of these stately white birds with their large summer needs for food. They would have had to share the fishing areas with many other marsh and shorebirds as well. Ospreys, herons, and egrets—all with hungry young—would have flown the tidal shores. Anhingas, cormorants, and brown pelicans—other fish-eating members of the Pelicaniformes order —would have competed for food.

With the scattering of colonies of white pelicans on lakes from British Columbia and Ontario in the north to Texas in the south there is plenty of food. On the northern breeding grounds the living is good.

In the early morning pelicans fan away from the colony in groups. They often fish together on the lakes. The birds arrange themselves in a semicircle facing shoreward. Then, as though at a signal, they rush

(*Bottom left*) Brown Pelican, (*center*) White Pelican feeding young

inward, flailing the water with wings and feet. Small fish are driven into the shallows, and the pelicans scoop up great masses of them in their large leathery beak pouches. The parents return to the colony heavily weighted. There they regurgitate small fish into their throat pouches. Into the yawning pelican mouths the babies stick their heads and feed ravenously till all the food is gone.

By fall the young pelicans can fly. Now adults and babies leave the colonies and move southward through interior valleys of large rivers in long lines or V-shaped formations. The front birds act as a wedge, and those that follow fly more easily. Leaders are changed often, the hardest work being shared by members of the flock.

The trip is not hurried as with many birds. The pelicans feed and linger in many places. Occasionally they seem to take time to play. Thermals—or circular winds—rise over unevenly heating land and water, and the pelicans ride upward on them. As the birds circle into sun and away, the light glints and retreats from the brilliant white bodies. To a watcher it appears like magic as the birds appear, then disappear again and again. Occasionally, with rigid, half-closed wings,

Anhinga, or snakebird, feeding young

a bird dives, then swoops up again as it nears the ground. There is a thunderous sound of feathers vibrating. Sometimes a number of birds follow the dive of the first.

White pelicans end their migration along the warmer seas. On the South Atlantic and Gulf coasts they are fairly common all winter. Some are found in Southern California. Most birds leave again by the beginning of March, but some do not. A few linger until late spring, while others may remain all summer. Those that stay are believed to be nonbreeding birds. The nesting colonies lie in the open lands to the north.

Migration is a dangerous and exhausting part of a bird's life. Hundreds of millions of the migrants never reach their destination. Winds blow them out to sea; fogs confuse them; lighted towers and other buildings attract them to crash and die; high-tension and telephone wires trip and kill them in the dark. Those that do reach the wintering grounds often are thin and worn. Despite these negative facts, a majority of North American bird species migrate. The seasonal movement offers them unique advantages that offset the high costs.

For animals that remain in a cold climate, living is difficult. Storms and freezing cold chill bodies even through a ruffled feathery coat. To maintain high body temperatures, more food is needed than in warmer weather. At the same time there is much less available to eat. With the first heavy frosts most insects are killed. Fruits, berries, and seeds fall beneath the packing of snow.

Many of the birds that remain change their food and living habits. For example, the sage grouse eats insects during the summer, but in winter its diet is the blue-green sage leaves which remain alive. In addition, grouse escape the coldest weather by diving deeply into the snow, where winds and lashing cold cannot reach them.

Migrating birds can escape the difficulties and small food stores of winter. They enjoy two summers and no winter each year. This is a great bonus for animals that need such large amounts of high-energy foods. On the warm wintering grounds they often pack together in high concentrations. Territorial urges usually are forgotten. In the nonbreeding season less food is needed, and there is enough for all. Flocks often feed and sleep together, giving one another protection through numbers.

A few birds make very short migrations. Some move only from harsh upper slopes to more protected parts of the valleys. Many ducks make two migrations. In August they go to sheltered marshy places. There

1. European Cormorant 2. Wandering Albatross 3. Pelagic Cormorant 4. Gannet
5. Brandt's Cormorant

MIGRATION FLIGHT
(*Left*) Arctic Tern, (*center top*) Barn Swallow, (*center bottom*) Bobolink, (*right*) Golden Plover

all the flight feathers molt at once. The birds cannot fly on longer winter migration until new feathers have grown. The distance traversed by pelicans is small compared to many other birds. Bobolinks may fly 7,000 miles; barn swallows, 9,000.

The Arctic tern holds the record for long distance. This graceful white bird nests in the far north. As the northern days shorten, it leaves the breeding grounds. The rest of the year is spent 10,000 miles away in the Antarctic seas. Some of the birds travel through the Pacific; others go by the west coast of Europe and Africa. The golden plover travels almost as far. Some spend summer on the Arctic tundra and winter on the pampas of Argentina. Others fly across the 2,000 miles of open ocean from Alaska to Hawaii.

Almost nothing is completely predictable or general in migration. Some birds seem to be triggered by external things, the amount of daylight and the weather starting them on the way. As winter retreats, they follow. Mid-April to early May, arrival on the breeding ground may differ by two or three weeks each year. Other birds, such as warblers, are instinctual migrants. A very precise internal clock begins their twice-yearly trip.

There is a great variation in exactly how each bird species migrates. Most travel at not more than 3,000 feet above the earth. Some move at brush level. A few species have been found by radar at 5,000 to 14,000 or even 20,000 feet above the earth. Small birds seldom fly at more than 30 miles per hour, but swallows and starlings are faster. Hawks may migrate at 30 to 40, shorebirds 40 to 50, and ducks at 50 to 60 miles per hour. At these rates migrants may cover hundreds of miles each day or night. Some rest on the journey; others do not. Those birds that fly nonstop usually build up a large store of fat before beginning. Other birds move along in a more leisurely fashion and feed as they go.

Many birds have an inherited mental map. Most do not need to learn a migration route. Even young birds travel great distances without adult guides. Those that fly at night use the positions of the stars to orient themselves. Birds that move by day use the position of the sun in a similar way. Those migrants that travel both day and night seem to switch easily from one navigation system to another. In cloudy weather both night and day fliers may become confused.

Learning does play a part in the migration of some birds. Older geese and other waterfowl seem to "remember" landmarks during daylight. They lead the way for younger birds. Pigeons raised underground cannot find the way home. How birds pinpoint goals has never been explained. Possibly they are much more sensitive to the differing magnetic fields or to the forces created by the spin of the earth. Neither of these ideas has been proved, but neither has been shown wrong. No one knows.

People who studied birds used to speak of flyways, or the routes of greatest migration. Recent research has disproved the idea to an extent. All over the United States all night during migration people with telescopes watched the moon. The numbers of birds that crossed its glowing disk were counted: geese, bobolinks, sandhill cranes. Many radar stations cooperated by reporting the movements of migrants. As a result, we now know that birds seem to fly over most of the land areas. A majority of the smaller species travel on broad fronts at night. Only in the day do they mass in flocks or follow narrow pathways. In the spring such birds "swim" north on the warm air masses from the south. In the fall the process is reversed. They flow south on the cool winds of the north.

There are probably many answers to the riddles of migration rather than one. It will take a long time to dig out all and put them together.

SHORE BIRDS 1. Great Black-headed Gull 2. Lesser Black-backed Gull 3. Glaucus Gull
4. Common Tern 5. Herring Gull 6. Arctic Tern 7. Roseate Tern

13
Shore Song

The natural world is a patchwork of habitats, or different types of places in which animals live. Deserts, arctic plains, and deciduous forests all are large habitats. Inside these big areas there are smaller and smaller subdivisions. Each habitat differs from others in many ways. For large areas there are very obvious differences such as climate, form of land, and vegetation. Some of these factors present special problems that an animal must be able to overcome. Each also offers living things special advantages.

Animals and plants have not only habitats but also niches. A niche is the "occupation" of a living thing. In some habitats there may be many ways in which a living is made. Birds may eat insects, fish, plants, or each other. If they feed on the same thing, they may do it in different ways.

The number of birds that can live in any one place differs greatly. If there is lots of food and many hiding places and nesting sites, the carrying capacity is high. This means that many more birds and other animals may live in the area than in another place of a similar size.

The needs for life are never found in unlimited amounts, however. No matter how rich and varied a habitat, there are only a certain number of creatures that may live in it. This results in competition for life requirements. Those living things that fit an area best are most successful. Those that remain are particularly well adapted by their body form and the manner in which they live.

Five A.M. A thin beginning of light shows where land and sea meet. Overhead there is a loud cry. *Wock-wock-wock!* Black-crowned night herons are on the way to roost after a night of feeding on the shallows of the bay. With each breaker, water flows higher and higher on the sand. The tide is moving inward. In another hour it will be full.

The ocean beaches are relatively harsh and sterile places. Great and steady is the power of the waves. The beach shifts endlessly. A mix of sand and water prevents the growth of most water plants and animals. Here there are no pools of sweet life-sustaining water. The winds usually blow and sweep the sky of insect life. The evidences of death and destruction are more obvious than those of life. Wooden planks or broken limbs are bleached and beached after long drifting. There are piles of dried seaweeds or kelp and empty shells of many animals that have died in deeper waters. Stranded jellyfish shimmer dead in the sun. Occasionally there are decaying fish. It is hard to imagine that birds could live here. Yet they do.

The shorebirds are grouped together in the order Charadriiformes. In addition to the sandpipers and their close relatives, this classification includes the gulls, the terns, and the plovers. The plovers at first glance look a good bit like sandpipers. It is easy to tell the two groups apart, however. Plovers have pigeonlike bills and long legs. The sandpipers and their allies have thin, straight or slightly downcurved bills that almost always are as long as the head and sometimes much longer. It is on the rising tide that most of the beach birds feed.

The sandpipers and plovers have the same habitat for part of each day and part of each year. There are many different niches, however. The sandpipers, plovers, and their relatives are uniquely but differently fitted to capture the hidden life on the ocean shores.

The sanderlings have been named beach birds. These small, twinkling-legged, rapid creatures blend so well into their background that they are difficult to see when motionless. They are seldom found anywhere but on ocean beaches. Least sandpipers, semipalmated sandpipers, and ruddy turnstones are their constant companions. In addition, many other birds feed around them during migration, then scatter inland.

Sanderlings are the lightest-colored of the sandpipers. In flight they move with rapid, steady wingbeats. They turn and wheel in unison. There is no obvious leader and no regular formation. No one knows exactly how these birds keep their coordinated flying forms. On the beach sanderlings gather in large, loose flocks. With jerky rapid pace they swing rhythmically back and forth with the sweep and retreat of the waves. Although they may snatch some food from the incoming waves, these birds usually dig vigorously in the wet sand. With partly

70   ·

BEACH BIRDS 1. Black-bellied Plover 2. Spotted Sandpiper 3. American Golden Plover
4. Pectoral Sandpiper 5. Semipalmated Sandpiper 6. Broad-billed Sandpiper

open bill they probe a series of six to twelve holes that may be up to an inch deep. Sand fleas, shrimp, tiny crabs, and other small crustaceans are their major food.

The least and semipalmated sandpipers seem two different sizes of the same bird, although there are many minor differences. Mixed flocks run along just above the wave line and retreat rapidly as the waters advance. The heads of these tiny birds are constantly downward. With long, thin bills they probe the sand for beach fleas, worms, and tiny clamlike animals.

Spotted sandpipers jerk their tails up and down with every step. They feed mainly on flying insects. Flies abound among the windrows of seaweed. Upon these the spotties creep with slow, catlike steps. Occasionally they also feed on fish. When frightened, spotties flee with their easily recognized downturned wings and *peet-weet* call.

In breeding plumage turnstones are easy to spot. The upper parts are bright chestnut, the underparts white. Often their fast-moving legs seem only a blur of orange. They are very aggressive birds. With a hunched, threatening style they chase other turnstones as well as many other shorebirds. As their name indicates, turnstones turn over rocks and other debris to hunt snails, crustaceans, insects, and shellfish. Small objects are turned with the bill; larger ones are pushed over with the breast and full weight of the bird. They are energetic feeders. As they root in debris, bits of shell, moss, or sand may be thrown seven to eight inches into the air. During low tide they dig holes in the sand big enough to hide a man's fist.

The plovers are seen most often during migration. In the spring the coal-black throats of black-bellied plovers stand out against the tawny sand. On the beaches they run swiftly along the water's edge. Often they stop to look about or strike at some bit of food. The semipalmated plover also migrates day and night along the shore. Although they may be very common, these birds are hard to see. Their plumage matches the wet sand almost perfectly. Like ghosts, they run with erect, head-up postures and in a helter-skelter fashion. Up the beach and down, left, then right, they jab out swiftly at food. Often they pause and stand still or jerk and bob their heads.

The shy oyster catchers also belong to the shorebird group. Occasionally they are found near rock jetties. With their long, blunt, bright-red, flattened bills they chisel limpets, mussels, and oysters from the rocks. These birds easily twist open the shells to eat the soft, salty parts inside. On broad sandy beaches they probe to the full length of the bill. They pat wet sand vigorously with their feet to drive up and out insects, worms, or other sand-living creatures.

SHORE BIRDS (*Left*) Oyster-catcher, (*right*) Ruddy Turnstone

Both gulls and terns fly along the beaches but usually make their livings in very different ways. They share the same habitat but have different occupations within it.

The terns are smaller animals. With heads bent downward in watching, they fly with slow, graceful wingbeats along the clear edge waters, diving after minnows and other small fish. Gulls occasionally fish, but more often they are scavengers. They hunt for the dead, the nonmoving, or the slower land creatures. Birds' eggs, beached fish, grasshoppers, mice, and scraps thrown from fishing boats are a few of the foods that make up their diets. Like many birds that feed on the ocean, gulls have nasal salt glands. Too much salt in the body would be deadly. For ocean-feeding birds, the kidneys cannot remove enough. The nasal glands excrete and concentrate the extra salt. Tearlike droplets roll down the beak and away.

Behind the wind-built dunes and only a short way from the ocean, a very different world exists. Here the shoreline jags inward. There is a protected bay. A salt marsh surrounds it. Here a variety of grasses and reeds grow. On the higher ground there are trees. Large areas riddled with fiddler crab holes spread from the shoreline. Waterless flats ap-

(*Left to right*) Sora Rail, Clapper Rail with chick, Virginia Rail

pear with each low tide. Oysters, worms, crabs, clams, snails, and many, many other creatures burrow in the dark, thick mud. In this quieter abundant world there is room for more birds than those of the shore. Their lives follow a quieter rhythm of the sea.

In the tight clumping of grasses are marsh wrens and seaside, Savannah, and sharp-tailed sparrows. There are many insects on which they feed.

Among the dark-green reeds live more specialized marsh birds. The Virginia, clapper, and sora rails are chickenlike creatures that lead hidden, solitary lives. Their calls cackle, whinny or clap, but the birds rarely are seen. The thin, sideways-compressed bodies slip easily and quickly through the marsh grass, weeds, and underbrush. Their stout medium-length legs and long toes allow them to move rapidly on the marsh terrain. All seem to fly only weakly, reluctantly, and for short distances, but the sora and Virginia migrate. All swim and dive with ease. With the ebb of the tide, rails advance toward the sea. Incoming water returns them to the bank. Day and night they feed on fiddler crabs, snails, fish fry, insects, and plants.

74

Low tide is the time of feeding for many of the salt marsh birds. Some of the beach birds come inland at this time. Spotted sandpipers and black-bellied plovers dabble in the sticky mud. Willets, lesser yellowlegs, and long-billed curlews are drawn to the abundance of food. Slowly and sedately these birds stalk across the mud flats or wade to the full length of their legs in the shallows. Aquatic crustaceans, mollusks, grasshoppers and other insects, small fish, and worms are the food source of all.

The yellowlegs finds its food on the surface of the mud or the water. Only rarely does it probe with its slender, delicate bill. The food-finding technique of the curlew is very different. Its long, curved beak probes full length into mud and sand. The ends have separate controlling muscles that allow a fingerlike pinching and opening. Many nerve endings allow the bird to feel its food in the mud. With such equipment it is easy to find deeply hidden worms, shrimp, and young insects. In addition, the curlew eats a wide variety of foods in different places. During the day it is in the marshes. At night it wades easily in and out of the surf. During breeding season it lives in upland areas. Crawfish, crabs, snails, periwinkles, toads, worms, insect young, grasshoppers, crickets, beetles, caterpillars, spiders, flies, butterflies, berries —all form part of its food.

The herons and egrets and bitterns are also wading birds of the salt

SALT MARSH BIRDS (*Top to bottom*)
Willet, Long-billed Curlew, Lesser
Yellow-leg

marshes. Their necks and legs are long, the beaks usually straight and forcepslike for grabbing fish. All the members of this order—Ciconiiformes—have one very obvious peculiarity. Their neck vertebrae are of unequal length. This forces the birds to carry their necks kinked into an S shape when flying and often when at rest.

For the herons and egrets that live in the salt marshes, there are many ways of living. The bitterns have brownish-streaked bodies that blend well among the reeds in which they live. Their eyes are placed low on the head; seeing down into the water while fishing is easy. In case of danger these rooster-sized birds freeze with bills pointed upward. They remain so quiet and move so little that it is almost impossible to see them. In the spring they call with a guttural gulping, belching, braying, and booming. They are often called "thunder pumper" or "stake driver."

Each of the day-active herons and egrets seems to have a slightly different method of feeding. With its head extended far outward on a long neck, the great blue stalks slowly in the shallows. At other times it simply stands still and waits. A fish swims by within reach. It is

76

WADING BIRDS 1. Common large Egret 2. Great Blue Heron 3. Green Heron 4. Cattle
Egret 5. Black-crowned Night Heron 6. Snowy Egret

grabbed, flipped upward, and swallowed quickly. The great blue eats many things besides fish. Among the tall grasses these large birds search for frogs, snakes, lizards, birds, and mice. The snowy swishes its golden feet about in the water, then snatches the small fish and shrimps that have been so disturbed. These dainty white birds may feed in groups. The gray and reddish-tan Louisiana is very common. Stealthy and alone, it stalks small fish, worms, and snails on the salt marshes or hunts in freshwater areas for tadpoles, leeches, and slugs. A feeding reddish egret seems almost to have gone mad. It runs about in a frenzied fashion while stabbing at the fish that it chases. The green heron often stays on the bank among the vegetation. It grabs fish that swim too near.

For a bird that does not get totally wet, fish eating can be a sloppy, slimy business. To help solve this problem, the herons and egrets have a peculiar type of feather called powder down. The powder downs are never shed and grow continually from the base throughout life. On the bare spaces of breast and rump and flanks they are present in well-marked paired patches. Herons and egrets rub their heads on the patches after eating. The tips of the specialized feathers fray into a powder that soaks up slime and dirt. All herons and egrets have a middle toe with comblike serrations. This built-in tool is used for grooming after eating and powdering is done. Powder downs are found in other groups of birds but are not so well developed or used as by these long-legged birds of the marshes.

The tide again flows high to the shore. On waters quiet and deep new birds appear. Ducks and coots, cormorants and anhingas—all dive after fish in the deeper waters. Ospreys and bald eagles sweep low across the bay. Both of these birds are opportunistic. They will feed on almost anything. Ducks, coots, fish, mice—all may be snatched up and eaten.

With lower bills extended into the water, black skimmers cut criss-crossing lines in the bay. They flip up and eat small fish and other aquatic creatures. After every gulp the lower bills extend down again. Wear is great. Nature has made allowances for such a problem, however; the lower bill grows faster than the upper. It remains long and slender: an excellent scoop for fish.

Day after day, night after night, the rhythms of the ocean continue. On shore and in marsh birds move with the tides. Each finds its place in the pattern of survival.

14
Bird Brains

We have a large brain with many creases and folds. The outer part is called the cortex. It is used for learning and thinking as well as for other things. Birds have small, smooth brains. There is almost no cortex. This does not mean birds are stupid, however. The cortex of birds doesn't seem to have anything to do with intelligence. It is used for smell. In the windy sky where few odors stay very long, a cortex is not important. Bird intelligence seems to rely on a very different part of the brain.

Above the massive jutting of red rock hills and smoother weather-cut caverns of the Southwest the raven soars. In a land large, yet scarce of life it makes its living well. The stories of many of the native American peoples of the area use this bird as a model of great intelligence and wisdom.

In the East is a smaller, more widespread relative of the raven: the common crow. In the spring flocks of these crafty creatures descend on sprouting cornfields. With a jaunty, alert walk they pull up row after row of new plants. The eggs of quail, pheasants, and ducks also fall prey. Crows are given little credit for the tons of grasshoppers and other harmful insects they eat. Farmers and hunters have joined against them.

In many parts of the country crow hunting is an important sport. The communications of the birds are used against them. Crows have many different calls. Some cause flight. Others call the flock together. Imitation crow calls summon the gregarious birds. They are shot as

they gather. Many birds are killed at night when they roost in large numbers.

Despite the many dangers of crow life, these birds survive with ease. Large numbers of babies are not produced. Crows escape the plots of their enemies by pure wit. Possibly the best proof of intelligence is success in withstanding persecution. If this is true, crows rate very highly indeed.

Let's visualize another bird in a commonplace situation.

A chicken has wandered outside a fence. When its companions are

80

fed, it wants to return. There is an open gate only a few feet away, but the chicken doesn't understand the gate is there as it runs frantically back and forth in front of the same stretch of fence. Occasionally it tries to squeeze through the wire. It may continue to act thus for a long time.

Are chickens stupid and ravens and crows smart? Deciding about the intelligence of birds or even humans is difficult. There are many ways to define intelligence. There are many different kinds of learning.

The behavior of a species helps it survive. Ways and places of living differ. Hence, in each bird or other animal, there is an inborn tendency to pay attention to some things that are important and to ignore others that are not.

Birds operate a good bit by instinct, or inborn behavior. Such ways of acting do not seem to involve much thinking or understanding. They are stereotyped, or rigid, and not easily changed by learning. Once triggered, instinctive behavior continues even if it no longer makes sense. For example, if newly hatched babies are placed in a nest still being built by tricolored blackbirds, the nestlings will starve to death. The adult birds continue to build the nest and ignore the frantic young.

All living things learn to some extent. One of the simplest types of learning is habituation. Birds and other animals simply learn what is meaningless to them and no longer react to it. For example, a blind left on a breeding colony of gulls will be ignored after a period of time.

Many birds learn by trial and error. At first a sparrow may eat any seed or insect. Later it chooses those that taste the best. If thistles form an uncomfortable nest, a bird will not use them the next time. It is not always easy to tell how much of such changed behavior is due to learning, however. Many older birds fly better than younger. Is this because older birds have learned better techniques? Or is it because the nerves, muscles, and instincts have matured and are more capable of smooth action? No one knows.

Play aids learning. Falcons drop a mouse, then swoop down to grab it again. By such practice these birds learn the best ways of capturing moving prey.

Imprinting is a type of learning characteristic of chickens, geese, ducks, and other precocial young. It is simply a very fast and not reversible learning.

Between the thirteenth and sixteenth hour of life a mallard duck "learns" to recognize and follow its mother. At that time it will follow any moving object and in the future will consider it a parent. A mate will be selected to fit the parent model. Dogs, cats, cardboard figures, and humans all have played this role. A duck will ignore others of its kind if it imprints on another model. The critical period for imprinting is very short. By the twenty-ninth hour after hatching, imprinting no longer will take place. A similar but much slower learning may take place in altricial birds—or even humans for that matter.

The last type of learning is the kind we usually consider intelligence. Insight learning involves a sudden understanding of a problem or situation.

Some birds seem able to do this type of learning, and others do not. Herons sometimes fish by dropping bits of bread into the water to attract fish. Great tits in England learned to remove cardboard milk-bottle tops and drink the milk. The habit spread very rapidly as one bird imitated another. Canaries have "figured out" how to reach food suspended by a thread. The birds hold the thread with one foot and with the beak pull the prize closer and closer. Wild crows manage a similar trick with ice fishermen's lines. A bird grabs the line at the hole and walks backward five or six feet. It then steps on the line so it will not slip back and walks on it toward the hole. Once again it grabs the watery cord and walks backward. After a number of "pulling trips" the fisherman's bait pops onto the ice and the crow eats it.

Recent studies show some birds have relatively large abilities to learn. Crows, ravens, magpies, myna birds and parrots all are very good at reverse learning. This means they can learn to pick a circle to get a food reward after they have learned to pick a square. Rats have a much more difficult time mastering the task. In another learning test which involved forming a theory of what was happening, even chickens outdid all mammals except monkeys and apes. Canaries could pick from a group the object that was different. Ravens and parakeets easily count to seven. There were learning problems that animals considered intelligent, such as elephants and cats, could not solve while crows, ravens, and their relatives quickly figured out the answers.

There is still a lot of research for scientists to do, to help understand both birds and humans. Even at this point it appears that "bird brains" differ a good deal. With respect to some birds at least, it might not really be such a bad name to be called.

15

An Eye Looks Down

Both the Strigiformes, or owls, and the Falconiformes, or hawks, falcons, and vultures, are birds of prey. Both groups seek animal food. They have bodies specialized in various ways for this life-style. The feet of most of these hunting birds are of a strong, grasping type. The beaks are hooked and powerful. Easily they rip the flesh of rabbit, mouse, or bird. Pellets are thrown back up through the mouth. They contain indigestible remains such as teeth, bones, and hair.

Once hawks and owls were classified together. Now scientists believe they are not very closely related. Owls are more like goatsuckers, parrots, nighthawks, and poorwills while hawks and vultures are related to herons. There are a number of obvious differences between these two groups.

Most owls hunt at night while the Falconiformes are creatures of the day. Owls all have large eyes that face forward in a special disk of feathers. Their heads are big; the necks seem short. Owl plumage is soft and fluffy. Silently they move through the air. Diurnal, or day-time, birds of prey may have some of these traits, but none have all.

United States Falconiformes include vultures, ospreys, accipiters, broad-wing hawks, eagles, kites, and falcons. Vultures differ from most others of this group. Usually they eat dead animal foods. The beaks and feet are considerably weaker than those of its close relatives. Condors—the largest flying birds in the world—are vultures.

Vision is particularly important for birds of prey, but their unusually good sight is mostly a matter of degree. All birds are eye-brained

BIRDS OF PREY (*Top left*) American Osprey, (*top right*) Swallow-tailed Kite, (*bottom*) Eastern Goshawk

animals. They gain more information from their eyes than from all other sense organs put together.

The structure of the bird eye is similar to that of other vertebrates. Its perfection comes from abundance of parts. The fovea of the eye is the point of sharpest vision. Humans have one fovea. Birds may have as many as three in each eye; some have a horizontal streak or large central area. Rods and cones are the light-sensitive cells in the eye. In birds they are extremely numerous and tightly packed. Cones are most common in day birds; rods in night fliers. The tight packing of rods in owl eyes allows a very great sensitivity to light, but they cannot see in *total* darkness any more than we can. Owls can see well at a hundredth of the minimum light intensity necessary for sight in humans, however.

The position of the eyes varies greatly with different birds. Plant-eating birds, such as ducks, quail, and doves, have eyes on each side of the head. Pigeons can see 340 degrees—almost anything but their own bodies. Hawks and other predators need to focus in front. They have eyes directed forward. The eyes of owls are nearly as frontal as ours, but they cannot move. To make up for this, owls can turn their heads almost completely around.

There are some specializations in the eyes of birds. Colored oil droplets are present in the cones. With these built-in haze-piercing filters birds can see better on misty days. The contrast of colored objects is also increased. As birds sweep hungry over the land, food items seem to blink on and off like tiny lights.

Humans have an upper and lower lid. Birds have a third called the nictitating membrane. This extra lid protects the eye. Like a windshield wiper, it cleans the undersurface of the eyelids and brushes the cornea with tears at every flick. In most birds the nictitating membrane is used for blinking; the eyelids close only for sleep. Normally the lower lid raises up and the upper lid remains immobile. In owls the upper lid is used to wink, however, and both lids close the eyes for sleep.

Hawks, eagles, vultures, and owls all have enormously large eyes. They receive images larger and sharper than do most animals. Focus is clear and fast. With their forward-facing eyes, hawks and owls probably have stereoscopic vision. Unlike many other birds, they see a large portion of their world with both eyes. The view is three-dimensional. Birds of prey have a better idea than most birds of the distance to any object.

BIRDS OF PREY (*Center*)
Snowy Owl, (*top left*)
Great Horned Owl, (*top right*) Burrowing Owl

It was early May. All night the male great horned owl had hunted. Again and again he swooped low over the flat gray-brown countryside. As he flew, he resembled a giant moth. His wings were long and wide and silent. They made barely a sound. As with all night-hunting owls, his plumage was velvety soft. Frilly, sound-deadening feathers edged his wings. Long ear openings almost girdled his head. Both in front and behind were flaps fringed with stiff feathers. They directed his hearing forward or backward at will. With such equipment the great horned owl could hear the smallest sounds of prey, yet not be heard himself. He could locate a mouse as well by sound as by sight.

On this night the moon was hidden. Small animals moved about more in the darkness. Hunting was good. In the velvety black the male owl had plunged silently to the earth or flown low and reached outward with his large, strong claws.

86

Mice and meadow voles were his prey. Some of the food he ate. Most of it he carried to his hungry mate. She did not hunt at all during the time of incubation. One egg remained. There were two quickly growing young. Baby owls cannot keep a steady body temperature when they are first hatched. The warm brood patch of the female must protect them from the cold. Only after the last egg has hatched and the babies are older will the mother owl hunt.

In the dim gray light of dawn the male owl returned to the nest. As he flew, the world over which he moved changed. The sage-covered flats sloped downward into a small green valley. Willows and cottonwood trees grew; water was plentiful. The nest was 20 feet high in a cottonwood tree. The male owl perched on a limb nearby, while he and his mate exchanged a few short *who-whoos*. He offered her a mouse. The young already were well fed, so she ate it herself in one gulp.

Soon the sun rose, and the normal activities of daylight began. A truck moved slowly down the road. Several children played ball in the high grass. A cat prowled about a deserted building. The owls did not seem aware of any of this. With eyes closed, motionless and silent, they appeared asleep. It was difficult to see the brownish gray body of the female on the nest. She seemed to blend almost perfectly with her background.

Turkey vultures are late risers. As the early-morning sunlight first spreads across the flat marshlands, there is no sign of these large dark birds moving V-winged in the sky. The night roost is a deserted fire tower. On it sit about thirty vultures. Their naked red heads flash bright against the morning sky. They spread their long wings away from the body and bask for as long as an hour. From front to back they turn, heat soaking into the dark bodies which night has cooled.

The heating of the ground is uneven. Warming currents of air rise over the land and spiral upward. On these the turkey vultures are dependent, for these two-toned brownish birds are masters of soaring. With a few heavy flappings they take off, then simply ride the circular winds upward. They are so skilled at using air currents that they may soar for hours without flapping a wing. At times they hunt from as high as 1,000 feet above the earth. Sometimes they glide only slightly above the trees. With careful eyes they scan the surface of the ground and watch other vultures. If one bird drops down to feed, others will follow. Vultures seem to have a much better sense of smell than most birds. They may use odor to help locate food.

(Left) Black Vulture, (top center) California Condor, (bottom right) Turkey Vulture

Vultures regularly patrol the intertwining concrete highways, which are good sources of food. In the darkness cars have killed many things: rabbits, a skunk, a badger, a deer. The vultures feed on these. If the food is plentiful, the large birds may gorge until they can no longer fly. Instead, they remain by the kill and wait for digestion to lighten their load. Frightened vultures may escape by throwing up the extra food. In their slow attempts to fly, some overstuffed birds are hit by cars— victims of the same source that fed them.

Many people think of vultures with horror. However, these birds do a great service in the natural order of life. The dead and decaying bodies of animals might spread disease. The smell of rotting would be much more common. Turkey vultures are janitors of the air. Because of them, the world is a healthier, more pleasant place for us all.

Golden eagles are a common sight in many areas of the West. In early spring these enormous birds court with an aerial dance. High above a dark jutting of lava cliffs a pair soars, calling to each other. The male is above the female. Suddenly he dives toward her. Upside down she rolls and grasps his feet with hers. Both birds keep wings fully outstretched. They cartwheel downward. Several hundred feet below they separate and fly upward again.

Bald Eagle, *(top right)* aerial courtship dance

Golden Eagle with young

Although eagles are excellent soarers, they often hunt from a perch. Silently they sit until a rabbit or some other small unaware creature scurries by. The eagle plunges on it with an extremely powerful grip. The three front claws paralyze and suffocate. The hind claw acts as a dagger. Death is swift.

Ranchers and sheepmen have killed many of these large wild birds. Poisons are planted. Hunters shoot the majestic birds from airplanes. They blame the eagle for killing large numbers of young sheep. Some unprotected lambs are taken, but the overall kill is not large. Golden eagles and hawks hunt only when hungry. They do not kill for pleasure. Gracefully and easily these large birds of prey glide over as much as 15,000 acres of home range. For birds of so wide a territory, food is easy to find. They do not feed exclusively or even very often on domestic animals. Rabbits, ducks, grouse, and frogs are a large part of the diet. In the winter golden eagles occasionally feed on carrion.

Killing golden eagles goes against the interests of the sheepman. For the rancher, these large birds do more good than harm. When eagles feed on the jackrabbits, grasses grow better. There is more food for all. Many states now have laws protecting golden eagles, but lawbreakers continue to slaughter them.

90

16

The High and the Low

Chicken life is far from democratic. In any group of hens there is a high bird and a low. All others fall somewhere in between.

The life of these two creatures is extremely different. The high-ranking hen moves in a slow and stately style. Her feathers are sleek and well groomed; her body is plump and healthy in appearance. She seems in no hurry to do anything; indeed, she need only raise her head and the wave of chickens breaks before her. She eats her fill whenever she wishes; none dares compete with her. By fighting one to one with all other hens in the flock, she has won her position—and all are aware of it. She may peck any other hen in the group, but none dare peck back. This status carries over into all areas of her life.

In the depressions where the chickens dust themselves she may pick any place she wishes and be given it. A choice of nest boxes is hers, and the center warmest spot on the nighttime roost. She is queenly and proud even to roosters. The cocks' wing-spreading, short-stepped dance about her often causes her simply to walk away. Most lower-ranking hens will squat as an invitation to mate. Her indifference does not mean she will not copulate. Rather, it causes the male to court her harder until at last her eggs are fertilized.

The life of the lowest hen is very different. She may peck no hen but may be pecked by all. Often she is driven about endlessly. In the early morning and late evening, when the feeding trough is not in use, she skitters to it and gulps her food desperately. Any minute a hen might arrive and chase her away. Fevered and frightened, she makes false starts and runs, expecting danger even when there is none. At night she dares only hover on the edge of the roost. When the temperatures plunge to below freezing, she shivers alone. If any rooster approaches with his mating dance, she squats immediately in an invitation to mate. It is not hard to recognize this sorry hen. She has a beaten, numbed appearance. Her head stays lowered, her wings hang, and her body feathers are ruffled and unpreened.

Between the high and the low there are many degrees of peck order or dominance structure. Each bird knows her place in the social world of chickens. One bird may peck two others but be pecked by four herself; another may peck five birds and be pecked only by the top-ranking hen. Roosters usually do not peck hens. If there is more than one male, they have their own ranking system. A dominant rooster may prevent other males from mating. Some of the lower-ranking roosters become totally beaten down by this system. Even when all other cocks are removed, they dare not mate.

The peck order in chickens arises slowly in flocks that grow up together. Downy chicks already threaten each other but don't peck. As they grow a bit older, the real fighting begins. By ten weeks after hatching the peck order is set up.

When groups of strange adult hens are brought together, there is a flurry of fighting. Each hen squares off with another. A few in poor health, lacking fighting ability or aggressiveness, are destined to low positions. They may not fight at all but run and assume positions that show they are submissive, or willing to be dominated. While the fighting for position goes on, there is severe disruption in the chicken yard. Even chickens that will be the higher-ranking are bedraggled and wounded. The birds often lose weight and stop laying eggs. When the social structure is again set up, fighting almost ceases. A raised or lowered head is usually enough to remind others of position. Now chicken life goes back to its normal ways. Hens dust, lay eggs, mate, and feed. For the low-ranking chickens life is far from pleasant, but for the group the world is serene.

There is no happy ending to this story unless humans step in. This they have done to study the psychology of chickens.

Hens were injected with rooster sex hormones. Low birds became much more aggressive or willing to fight. They began to attack their "superiors" and rapidly rose in the social group.

Other hens were switched from group to group. Chickens had very poor memories for peck orders. After only a two-week separation from a stable group a whole new round of fighting began. Scientists discovered hens had different positions in different groups. A bird might be high in one group of very submissive chickens, middle in a second different group, and even among the low in a group selected for size and aggressiveness. A single new hen placed in an established group had an almost impossible task before her. To establish her position, she had to fight every hen in the group. No matter how healthy and aggressive she was in the beginning she had a difficult time gaining anything other than a low rank.

There are many groups of mammals, such as monkeys and dogs, that have social relationships resembling those of chickens. Each animal has a social position with respect to other animals and knows it. Many people have seen an uncomfortable resemblance to human ways.

SEA BIRD COLONIES 1. Razor-billed Auk 2. Common Guillemot 3. Dovekis 4. Common Murre

17
Cities of Birds

Many groups of birds nest in large colonies. There are advantages because large numbers of birds protect one another. It is more difficult for a hungry animal to sneak up on hundreds of birds than on one or two, for a warning cry goes up quickly. Adults escape to breed again even if the young are lost. In other cases the whole colony may drive off predators; even if a few young are killed by enemies, many many others remain.

Birds in colonies also seem to stimulate one another. The courting of one pair of birds encourages others in the same activity. The whole colony stays synchronized. Egg laying takes place at about the same time for all the birds. A larger number of young of the same age survive.

Gull colonies are a well-known type of bird city, but there are many others. Herons and egrets nest together in colonies called rookeries. They are often joined by brown pelicans and anhingas. Many of the ocean birds such as auklets, murres, guillemots, albatrosses, and penguins nest in large colonies.

In a cove of a large northern lake there is a small oval island. It is only a short distance from the shore, but the water is deep. Few creatures without wings cross the stretch of cold and dark.

All late fall and winter the world of the island seems empty. Only jackrabbits and sage grouse live there. Occasionally a magpie flies to a tree on its edge, or flocks of geese and ducks land nearby. Snow falls steadily. It piles up deeply on the small piece of land in the lake.

One day in early March there is a change. A group of about a hun-

(Bottom left) Common Tern with chicks. In the courtship offering *(top right)* the male presents fish to the female.

dred large gray and white birds circles high in the sky. The sunlight flashes brightly on their white feathers. There is the sound of clear buglelike calling. Suddenly the birds glide down toward the island. They seem about to land but at the last minute swoop upward. Again and again the birds rise into the air, then glide down toward the island. Each time they seem about to land. Each time they swoop up at the last minute.

After about fifteen minutes the birds seem to grow tired of the swooping, rising flight. They disappear over the crest of a nearby field. For a long while the cries can still be heard.

The birds are gulls, and the island is their nesting colony. For all the winter the birds have been spread out over the surrounding land. They have fed on dead fish on the lakeshore, garbage at a dump, or the animals killed by cars on the road. During this time each gull has lived alone.

96

Now all that is changing. The longer days have caused the physical changes of the breeding season. The birds feel a sudden need to behave differently from the way they have through the short gray days of winter. In this way instinct speaks to them. Each bird moves back toward the island.

For many days after the gulls first return they do not land. They circle and call. They glide down and up again. It is another two weeks before the birds at last come to rest on land. The period of indecision is over. The days are becoming long and warm. It is time to pair and to mate: to build nests, lay eggs, and raise young.

About 15,000 gulls breed on the small island. By early April the colony is well under way. The male gulls first gain ownership to a piece of land. They posture, give loud trumpeting calls, and threaten one another by body position. The bird with neck stretched up, bill pointed down, wrists of wings pushed forward and eyes half closed is a bird of which others are wary. His stance is not sleep or relaxation. It is threat. A resting bird takes a very different pose. Its neck is drawn in, the wings tucked away.

At the beginning of the season fights are common. In tug-of-war or pulling fights each bird tries to pull its opponent across the territorial boundaries. Other fights are more violent. Both bill and wings are weapons. The fighting gulls try to peck each other from above. When one bird has another down, the top male uses his half-folded wing as a club. Occasionally a bird wants both to attack and to flee. He solves the problem by doing neither; he redirects his activity and pulls grass instead.

After the territories are established, the females arrive. Gulls mate for life, but the tie must be restrengthened with each breeding season. In addition, young males and females must find mates.

Approaching a territorial male is not a simple business. When a female lands near an unmated male, he gives his long call. Two drives war within him. He is attracted to the approaching female, and at the same time he wants to attack and drive her away.

The female behaves as though she were aware of his problem. She uses appeasement behavior. All her actions signal to the male that she is not an enemy. She hunches her body, keeps the neck horizontal and her head withdrawn between her shoulders. Around and around she walks, with each circle coming closer to her prospective mate. At last she begs by tossing her head and pecking at the base of his bill. If the male accepts her, he throws up some food. She eats. After several days of this courtship feeding the pair mate.

Despite the bond, all may not be harmony. Frustrated by his fights with neighbors, the male may attack his mate. By a wing tip or neck he grabs her and swings her around.

The female does not know the territorial boundaries at first. She learns these by watching the male. After a while she too takes part in the fighting. Neighboring females attack each other. Together male and female give the long call: a very aggressive trumpeting cry. As they stand against all other birds in this fighting, noisy city, their bond to each other is strengthened.

The male begins the search for a nesting site. He gives a wailing long-drawn-out cry called the mew call and begins to wander around the territory. The female follows him. At a site under a sage bush or in a hollow by a rock, the male bends forward. He bobs his head rhythmically while giving a muffled coughing sound, called choking. If his mate joins with him, the nest place is set. Day after day they will come here to mew and choke. With each visit the place of the nest is set more firmly in each bird's mind. In addition, the tie between mates is increasing in strength. Now they fly to and from the feeding grounds together. At last together they scrap a depression and weave straws or grasses in the rim.

With the laying of the first egg, the rhythm of life in the colony changes. Male and female no longer fly away together. If the egg is left alone, a neighbor will attack it. One adult always must remain as guardian. The birds take turns on the nest. They relieve each other with a ceremony of mewing, choking, or head tossing. Feeding and incubating take time. The fights between neighbors drop off. The colony settles to a temporary quiet.

Incubation continues for weeks. Near the time for hatching, the chicks already peep within the shells and the parents answer. When the alarm cry of kak-kak-kak spreads across the colony, the unhatched babies grow silent.

Hatching is slow, hard work. For as long as a day, the tiny egg tooth chips away at the wider end. At last the wet baby emerges. Within several hours it is dry and fluffy.

Between adult and newly hatched baby there are many instinctive signals. The chick is hungry. To get food, it pecks at a red spot on the parent's lower bill. The adult bird throws up.

A city of gulls is not a friendly or safe place for young. If left alone, they would be killed by neighbors. Babies that wander into a neighboring territory are pecked severely and often killed. The guarding of the nest continues, but no longer do eggs or babies need to be kept warm. The sun shines steadily; the island grows very hot. Overheating becomes a danger. Adult birds often shade the young or eggs. Male and female preen themselves often. There is a gland at the base of the tail. This is squeezed with the bill. Oil flows out and is transferred to the feathers. Almost all birds have preen glands and spend some time using them. The fluid keeps feathers in good shape. In addition, it contains vitamin D, which is swallowed during grooming. For a bird that spends time in the water, preening is particularly necessary.

A dog, a raccoon, a human—all are dangerous predators to a colony of gulls. The adult birds rise, screaming a warning cry. Babies scramble into hidden places and remain motionless. Most gulls simply circle. A few are more aggressive. With feet and wings they slam the intruder. Others throw up or defecate upon any creature foolish enough to enter the colony. As soon as the danger is over, parent birds alight and give the mew call. The danger is over. The young scramble back to the nest.

Baby gulls grow rapidly. They need a lot of food. The search begins at dawn. All day birds move in and out of the colony.

In early July some of the babies begin to bounce around while flapping their wings. By such practice the muscles and wings grow stronger. The young have grayish plumage and look very different from the adults.

By August the island again is deserted. The following year the same adult gulls will return. The babies will not. Among birds, gulls have an unusually long time until maturity. The young will be three or four years old before they reach adulthood. Then they will return to the same place in which they were hatched.

18
Bees of the Bird World

In a wild area of red and yellow trumpet-shaped flowers a male rubythroat has staked out his territory. This tiny creature—the only hummingbird in the eastern two-thirds of the United States—seems fearless in his defense of it. With a high, rapidly twittering voice and ferocious darts and dives he chases from his area crows, hawks, and even eagles, as well as other hummingbird males. Brilliant, hovering, jerking backward, forward, up and down, he sweeps over his territory with loudly buzzing wings. Alone he seldom makes any other noise.

His energy seems enormous, and his use of body supplies is equally great. He must constantly fuel this fast-burning furnace. The nectar of flowers is his source of instant energy. From plant to plant the small bird flies. His wings move so quickly they seem a blur. As he thrusts his long beak into the flowers, his facial feathers become dusted with pollen. It is transferred to the next blossom he visits. In this way hummingbirds fertilize flowers. Bees do the same thing in a similar manner.

There are special hummingbird flowers that are seldom visited by either bees or butterflies. Tubular, most often red and yellow, these flowers usually hang pendant or horizontal. With little or no landing area, it takes a tiny flash of a bird—hovering and long-billed—to tap them. Bees are not attracted to reds, but hummingbirds are. The bees and the birds compete very little for flower food. Probably the hummingbirds and their flowers evolved together.

Some people believe that hummingbirds instinctively choose red flowers; others argue it is the brilliant contrast of scarlet with green that attracts; still others say the birds simply learn to associate lots of

Ruby-throated
Hummingbird

food with a red color. Hummingbirds do not seem to stick to any particular color of garden feeder. They are able to tell tastes and sugar concentrations apart, however, and prefer some to others. This is unusual for birds. Most have very little sense of taste.

The hummingbird does not suck nectar through a hollow straw as once was believed. The tongue is long and double-grooved. Nectar flows slowly into the hollows. When the hummingbird pulls his tongue back into his mouth, he swallows as do most birds. Often insects are entrapped by the tongue. They form an important part of this tiny bird's diet. Nectar could not keep the hummingbird alive over long periods of time. Instead they spend part of their time actively hunting among the foliage of bushes and trees for bugs, flies, beetles, or wasps. Some birds sit in wait on perches. Like flycatchers, they dart out to capture insects.

Because of their small size and high-energy use even while at rest, hummingbirds lose heat very quickly. Some summer nights are too long and cold for these tiny birds to survive. The intense hummingbird must either feed constantly or slow fuel consumption in some way. It has solved the problem in an unusual way for birds. Each night it goes into torpor. As in longer hibernation, the body temperature

101

falls almost to that of the surrounding air. All the life processes slow down. The heart beats sluggishly. The breaths each minute are considerably less than in the waking state. At this greatly reduced living intensity the small body no longer needs as much energy to stay alive. Food stores last until a morning feeding.

Male rubythroats return first from the faraway wintering grounds. On migration they fly 500 miles nonstop across the Gulf of Mexico. To do so requires a great amount of energy. Before migration some hummingbirds add as much as 50 percent of their weight in storage fat. A scientist once carefully studied the energy needs of the bird for its overwater flight. He then figured how far the fat storage would allow a rubythroat to fly. His mathematical calculations indicated that the tiny hummers could not possibly make the trip. This hasn't bothered the birds, however. They continue to do so.

The females arrive several weeks later. For the male rubythroat this begins a new cycle of intense activity. His small, trim body—white below and glistening green on the back—sweeps in a ten-foot pendulumlike courtship arc before the female. When sunlight strikes his throat, it changes from black to a deep glowing orange or red. The wingbeats—always fast—now take on an amazing speed. Two hundred beats per second! The air fills with the high buzzing sound of air and feather meeting.

For a while the female watches his performance. Later she joins the flight. Like two tiny creatures riding an invisible seesaw, one rises, the other falls. Females lack the males' brilliant red throat, although in other ways the birds appear very similar.

When the courtship dance is done, the pair mate. Within the male's territory the female fashions a down and spider silk nest about one inch deep and one inch across. Into the minute cup she lays two pea-sized eggs.

The male drives away enemies but otherwise takes no part in the family life. Immediately after the courtship dance he loses interest in his mate. Instead, he courts other females and mates again.

The babies hatch naked except for very slight traces of down and grow on a diet completely composed of insects. This is a difficult time for the female bird. She constantly flashes away from the nest in search of food. Upon her return she may land, but usually she does not. Most often the mother bird feeds while hovering above her young. She sticks her long bill down the throats of the babies and regurgitates food.

When the young leave the nest at about nineteen to twenty-five days of age, they can fly well. This is essential, for hummingbirds can neither walk nor climb. Their feet are tiny and suited only for perching. To move even a few inches they must fly. The takeoffs are unusual, too. These "bee birds" leap up and carry the perch a short distance with them before release. As the bird resettles its weight on the branch, the tendons in the leg automatically tighten, as they do for all perching birds.

The flight of hummingbirds is easy to watch but not to see. They will come to artificial sugar water feeders readily. Some birds learn to respond to call and will perch on fingers of those who feed them. Despite this, hummingbird flight remained a mystery for a long time. The speed was too great. People could not be sure of what they saw or felt. Did these tiny sprites fly backward, or was it simply an optical illusion? Were fingers and branches pulled upward as a bird took flight, or was that only another case of imagination? It took a fast camera and lots of careful thinking to give answers and understanding for some of the strange observations. Hummingbirds *do* move backward. During hovering, the wings beat about fifty-five times per second, which means the tips move at about 20 miles per hour. As the bird backs, the beats increase to sixty-one per second, then seventy-five a second as the bird moves straight ahead.

There are a number of specializations in hummingbirds that allow their unusual flight and rapid wingbeats. Some of these characteristics they share with swifts—fellow masters of the aerial life. Both families of birds are grouped in the order Apodiformes. The name means without feet. Both groups have very tiny, seldom-used appendages. Their flying equipment is very effective, however, and more than makes up for the little-used feet.

The flying muscles of hummingbirds are enormous in comparison to the whole bird. They make up 25 to 30 percent of the body weight. Attachment to a breastbone or keel is proportionally deeper and sturdier than for any other bird. The powerful structure, plus the small size of the hummingbird, allows its wings to move faster than those of any other flying creature. In addition, the wing joint is swiveled in an unusual way. The wings thrust against the air on the upstroke as well as on the down. This is the secret of hovering and backing. In both cases the bird stands almost vertical in the air. Its tail points downward and slightly forward. The wings force the air first forward and the bird backward. On the return half stroke, the whole wing is rotated at shoulder joint so the upper surface strikes at the air, pushes down, and balances gravity.

There are 319 species of hummingbirds. All are located in the West-

(*Left to right*) Giant Hummingbird (largest hummer), Sicklebill Hummingbird (curved bill), Sword-billed Hummingbird (longest bill), Bee Hummingbird (smallest hummer)

ern Hemisphere, and all are small. The largest is the giant humming-bird of the Andes Mountains in South America. This biggest of the small is only 8½ inches and 20 grams in weight. Its wings move slowly enough that they can be seen in flight. Many are brilliant in color. In the past large numbers of hummingbirds were killed for jewelry mak-ing. In addition, strange and specialized dangers await the tiny hum-mer. Birds become caught in spiderwebs and stuck on thistles. They are eaten occasionally by dragonflies, fish, frogs, and nighthawks.

Hummingbirds are not the only birds that gather nectar. The honeycreepers and honey eaters also do this. However, no other bird feeds on nectar so exclusively or gathers it in flight. Beaks and tongues differ from one hummingbird to another, but all are modi-fied for getting nectar from flowers. All the bills are slender, thin, and pointed. Most are straight, although a few curve gently up or down. The sicklebill hummingbird is an extreme. Its bill is half-moon in shape. The South American swordbill is another type of extreme. Its bill is longer than the head, body, and tail of the bird put together.

104

19
Hunter of the Desert

The roadrunner is a bird now found exclusively on the south-western deserts. It lives in a world of extremes. The air is dry. Moisture does not smooth and modify the temperature. Nights are very cold and break suddenly to a violent daytime heat. There is little shade and even less water. For most of the year only stark, water-conserving plants seem to live. Cactus, greasewood, and yucca leaves are stiff, waxy-skinned, and unwilting in the brilliant sun.

In the early spring all this changes. Sunlight disappears and rain falls so heavily the ground cannot soak it all up. The runoff merges into deep, fast streams; flash floods crash along normally dry gullies.

Later there is an explosion of life. Plants and animals are everywhere. Small and dainty flowers bloom. Tortoise and rattlesnake, owl and kangaroo rat breed.

This time of living is intense and quick, however. The desert spring lasts only a short time. The heat returns; plants grow brown and seem to die. Again the world is harsh. For those that are active there all year round the adaptations must be great.

Roadrunners are in the order Cuculiformes, or cuckoos. Anis and the parasitic European cuckoo are relatives. All birds in the order are rather slender-bodied and long-tailed. All have medium to stout down-curved bills, rounded wings, and rather thick legs. The roadrunner has longer and stouter legs and a heavier bill than other cuckoos. Its plumage is a mix of white, buff, dark brown, and blackish green. The legs and feet are blue. A long horizontal strip of vivid orange and blue streaks behind the eye. When a roadrunner is excited, the strip of color becomes more visible. The dark head crest rises, the beak clicks, and the normally horizontal tail lifts almost to the vertical.

Television cartoons and comic books portray the roadrunner more as hunted than hunter. This is far from true. Roadrunners are occasionally pursued by coyotes and dogs, and these striped and fast-moving birds *do* appear to enjoy the chase. They are weak and reluctant fliers but can run up to 23 miles per hour and change direction with great speed. Quickly and easily they leave pursuers behind. Seldom are they caught.

It is as a hunter that the roadrunner is best known to those that share its desert world. Its feeding habits require strength, speed, and prowess. Snake killer, chaparral cock, lizard bird, ground cuckoo, cock of the desert, or simply little friend—all are names given as attempts to describe the life of the roadrunner.

If you go to the Southwest, you might hear the following story:

The roadrunner is a sly bird and a deadly untiring enemy of the rattler. Through patches of sunlight and of shade, in day and night alike, the crafty creature hunts. At last it finds a sleeping rattler. With silence and care, the bird builds a fence of cactus spines about the slumbering reptile. When the snake awakens, it attempts to escape. For many hours it batters itself against the solid frame. At last a great

Roadrunner

weariness fills the rattler. It ends its own life by impaling itself on the cactus spines or by biting itself to death.

The story is false, but it has a particle of truth. Snake killer *is* one of the nicknames of the roadrunner. Although it kills almost any type of snake and seems to prefer smaller, easier fare, this tough desert bird does occasionally kill and eat rattlers. The snake does not kill itself, however, nor is it entrapped in a hedge of thorns. The roadrunner fluffs its feathers. Again and again it darts at the snake. The rattler is fooled by the puffy shape of the bird. It strikes its venomous blows only into feathers. When the reptile grows tired, the bird moves in for a kill. It first pecks out the snake's eyes, then grasps the writhing creature behind the head. The roadrunner batters the rattler until it is dead, then swallows it head first. Most of its food is eaten in the same way.

Lizards, grasshoppers, spiders, wood rats, birds, and eggs—all are part of the diet. Some states have labeled the roadrunner a quail killer and placed a bounty on its head. These birds have an enormous appetite. They will eat almost anything living that is large enough to be seen and small enough to be swallowed in one piece. Ninety percent of its food is animal. The food-getting activities of these birds are often amazing. Roadrunners sometimes jump three to four feet into the air to capture swifts and swallows. One roadrunner grabbed a flying full-grown mockingbird, battered it to death, and swallowed it.

Roadrunners have a digestive apparatus powerful enough to handle this wide variety of food. Bones, hair, and feathers pass completely through the digestive tract. Like all birds, they have two stomachs. An unusually powerful muscular gizzard contains gravel and sand that rubs and breaks things. The other stomach is more like the human stomach. Digestive juices are secreted there and the breakdown of food begins. Unlike hawks, owls, and gulls, roadrunners do not throw up pellets of rough and undigestible parts.

As it moves, the roadrunner generates a lot of internal heat. Too high a body temperature can be fatal. Between hunting forays it rests in the shade. If the desert temperature rises too high, simply resting is not enough, however. For this active desert creature there must be other ways of cooling.

Birds do not have sweat glands. They cannot cool themselves by perspiring as we do. Many birds pant to cool themselves. The roadrunner has a slightly different technique that takes less energy. It is called gular flutter. Owls, nighthawks, and quite a few other birds do the same thing. A rapid local vibration begins in the chin. Air flows across the moist areas of the mouth and throat. Both water and heat are lost, and blood in the throat area is cooled by evaporation.

Roadrunners are difficult to watch. To the uninitiated, the roadrunner may be simply a scuttling sound in dry leaves, a glimpsed silhouette moving behind a rock, a long, slender creature flying quickly across a canyon or road before disappearing again into the desert terrain.

For those that lie in wait, a very different picture emerges. Here is an animal that sings with the rising sun in the spring. From a favored perch on an eastern rim of a mesa, the top of a dead tree, or high in a cactus, the male continues his harsh and throaty song for an hour or more. *Coo coo coo ooh ooh ooh. . . .* Gradually the voice lowers. When the bird begins singing, his head is low. As the notes fall, his head rises. The roadrunner often takes a sunbath between songs or at other times. He stands erect, shakes his feathers to loosen them, then soaks up the early-morning warmth.

Roadrunners have a number of calls. There are loud chuckling noises and soft purring sounds. The young open mouths with pink blotched linings and buzz as they beg for food.

The nest often is near the singing tree. Roadrunner cradles differ greatly one from another. The cup may be well hidden or easily seen. It might be in a low tree, a thicket, or a clump of cactus—from three to five feet above the ground, but rarely on it. Nests are created from snake skins, roots, mesquite pods, feathers, horse manure, and many other things.

Incubation is totally the job of the female. The male brings her food. She deposits her three to six chalky eggs at fairly long intervals. Incubation and development begin at once. The babies hatch at very different times. Fresh eggs, newly hatched young, and birds nearly full grown share the same nest.

It is a strange-looking group. The newly hatched young are featherless, greasy black creatures that resemble reptiles more than birds. They have only coarse, long whitish down. By the time the birds leave the nest they have the same plumage as the adults.

The female roadrunner guards her young well. If a predator comes too close to her nest, she pulls the well-known "injured bird" trick but with a difference. Most birds that lead away enemies pretend a broken wing. The female roadrunner drags her leg and falls over again and again. When the threatening animal has been lured far enough away, she recovers quite quickly. Almost instantly she races off among the desert brush.

108

20
Night Fliers

Nighthawks and their relatives in the Caprimulgiformes, or goat-suckers, order are very obvious birds. Most are not seen, however. By day they hide; by night they fly and feed.

It is their cries that draw attention. The calls usually are loud and repetitive. The whippoorwill, chuck-will's-widow, poorwill, and night-hawk all are called nightjars. The name fits well. The calls do jar an otherwise quiet night. Many native American legends deal with these birds. To the tribes along the Connecticut River the booming of the nighthawk was the shad spirit. It warned schools of these fish of the fate awaiting them farther upriver.

All the goatsuckers are night or dawn-dusk birds. All have tiny, insignificant feet that are almost useless on the ground. The enormous gaping mouths produced the legend that these birds milk goats during the hours of darkness.

Of the nightjars, the nighthawk is the most easily seen. Maybe you have stood in the twilight and watched the erratic, swiftly dipping and turning flight. The birds are probably feeding. As they sweep through the night, all types of insects are taken into the large, bristled mouth: moths, small flies, and mosquitoes. During swarms a lot of flying ants are eaten.

The flight of nighthawks resembles that of bats. In many parts of the United States the nighthawk is called bullbat. Both animals do feed exclusively on insects, but there the resemblance ends. Bats are mammals, and nighthawks are birds. A great gap separates the two.

You may see flocks of several hundred nighthawks during migration. On the long trek to Argentina these birds often fly near to the ground to feed. They may drink by skimming the surface of ponds and streams like gigantic swallows. Another nightjar—the poorwill—in the southern part of its range has the unusual habit of crawling into crevices and hibernating during the winter cold. Such a way of life preserves energy during a time of cold when there are few insects to eat.

The courtship flight of the nighthawk is easy to see. Over cities and farms, in the twilight or early dawn, the male flies in wide circles. Hidden, the female rests on the ground beneath him. Sometimes he hovers over her; at others he soars high above the proposed nest site. At approximately equal intervals he dives down to within a few yards of his mate, then swoops upward. At the bottom of the dive he throws his wings forward and down. Wind hits and vibrates the primary feathers. There is a loud whir. Later the displaying nighthawk lands near the female. He stands on his weak feet, spreads his tail like a fan, and wags it from side to side. His body rocks, and his throat puffs out. A white patch—normally invisible—becomes obvious. At the same time he gives a series of guttural croaking notes, but his mouth remains tightly closed.

Often the female seems unimpressed by her mate's exhaustive antics. She may ignore him or fly a few yards away. The male takes off again in his sweeping circles. His wingbeats are slow, broken by short periods of soaring. As he swings back and forth in the darkening air, he gives a buzzy nasal *peent* call. During nonmating season flocks of nighthawks fly together giving the same call. It probably helps the birds recognize one another and keeps large loose parties together.

After one of the aerial performances, mating takes place. This does not end the display flights, however, which continue through the incubation period. After the young hatch, the male helps with the feeding and the rocketing, whirring dives drop off. There are many other things to do.

Nighthawks, like other nightjars, are almost impossible to find in the day. Their plumage is a soft loose and fluffy mixture of browns and grays with darker streakings. It blends almost perfectly into its surroundings. On the ground or sitting lengthwise on tree branches, nighthawks remain motionless and perfectly hidden. Many people have been startled to have one of these birds fly suddenly from almost beneath their feet.

Eggs are as well hidden as adults. The female bird seems to prefer to lay them on gravel beaches or open barren areas of rock or soil. The eggs are never laid in forests. The flat graveled tops of buildings have

110

1. Whip-poor-will 2. Chuck-will's Widow. 3. Common Nighthawk 4. Chimney Swift 5. White Throated Swift

become a favorite nesting site in the city. There is no real nest. The eggs simply are laid in an unaltered spot. They have a great variety of markings and colors that aid camouflage.

Nighthawks are one of the few birds that move their eggs when disturbed. In the cavernous mouths, they carry them to some new safer place. Whole clutches may be moved accidentally also. The female drops swiftly onto her "nest." Each time the eggs may roll a few inches. Before hatching, the movement may be five to six feet.

Babies are fluffy and gray-mottled. They too blend into the background. For about twenty-five days the chicks remain near the nest area. Adults will defend them in a very owllike way. Male or female, they spread the wings, clack the bill, and stare steadily at an intruder.

Nighthawks are completely harmless to humans. Their name has caused them a lot of trouble, however. These insect-eating birds are not at all closely related to hawks, yet they have been blamed with them for killing chickens. Eggs have been destroyed, adults shot.

111

21
The Lone Fisherman

Kingfishers live in most places in the world. Polar regions and some oceanic islands are the few exceptions. These solitary, rattly-voiced birds belong to the order Coraciiformes. Most of the group are tropical or subtropical and many are very brightly colored. All have three front toes joined together for part of the length.

The belted kingfisher is the only coraciiform that lives in the United States. These strangely proportioned birds are easy to recognize. They seem top-heavy. The crested heads are large, the bills long and heavy. There is a short tail and tiny feet. The body is small. Belted kingfishers have gray-blue wings and a white collar. A chestnut-banded breast marks the female.

When moving from perch to perch, kingfishers fly close to the water in a distinctive way. A series of rapid wing strokes alternates with a short glide on half-closed wings. Clear woodland streams are a favorite home for belted kingfishers. Throughout the fall and winter months, these birds remain alone. With a strong swift flight and a harsh rattling cry all others of the species are driven away.

Within his territory the kingfisher has a number of favorite fishing spots. Most are limbs overhanging clear pools of water. In such a place a solitary bird usually perches for hours. When a fish appears, the bird usually dives after it at an angle. Occasionally it hovers 30 to 40 feet above the water, then plunges in a straight or spiral path downward. Sometimes the bird disappears completely beneath the waters for several seconds. The impact seems great. The kingfisher is uniquely fitted to withstand such shocks of a diving, fishing life. Its skull is very thick and hard. When the skilled fisherman reappears, it is usually with fish

Belted Kingfisher

in bill. It always returns to the perch before eating. There it beats the fish on the limb before swallowing it head first.

Despite its poor reputation as a trout killer, the kingfisher rarely takes such fish in the wild. Trout are too swift and well camouflaged. The gray-white bird feeds on the fish that man does not use. Chubs and dace, suckers and sculpins form the bulk of his fishy diet. When fish are hard to capture, the kingfisher eats many other things, such as crabs, crayfish, mussels, lizards, frogs, snakes, toads, turtles, young birds, mice, berries, salamanders, and grasshoppers and other insects. The indigestible remains of the fish and other animals do not pass through his digestive system. They are thrown back up in pellets.

In the spring kingfishers share their territory with a mate. Along a stream about three feet from the top of a bank of dirt, clay or gravel the male and female begin to dig. The hole is chiseled with the beak. The birds easily scoop loose dirt away with their three joined front

113

toes. Nest digging may take as long as three weeks or as short as a few days. The finished burrow is six feet long and slopes slightly upward. Near the end it turns abruptly. The nest cavity is an enlarged chamber. In it, on the bare ground, the female lays and incubates her six to seven eggs. The male brings food, and the female seldom leaves the cavity. Twenty-three days later the young hatch into a world that is almost totally dark.

The babies are blind, naked, and helpless. They have huge conical bills and reddish skin. For the first few days the female feeds them a dark-gray oily mass. Later the food is regurgitated fish.

The home of the baby kingfishers is an unusually safe and hidden place. They can take a long time to develop. The nestling stage is slightly different and longer in time than for most birds. For two weeks the babies' eyes remain closed. Sight gives no advantage in darkness, and the eyes might accidentally be injured. In a week sheathed feathers appear and gradually grow longer. The pinfeathers remain intact until the seventeenth or eighteenth day of kingfisher life. Suddenly all burst. Within twenty-four hours the young birds take on complete juvenile plumage. No longer do the babies resemble porcupines. Instead, they look very much like the adults. They are ready to fly and to leave the nest.

For a short time the babies stay close to their hatching place. During this time they learn to fish. Hunger is a spur. The female ceases feeding her young. Instead, she perches with them above the water. Again and again she dives upon a fish, beats it senseless, then drops it back into the water. The young watch it float away. At last the hunger becomes too great. One bird, then another plunges clumsily into the water. At first their aim is poor. Many hungry babies miss the fish and flutter about after it. With practice their fishing skills rapidly become better. Within ten days all the young are catching live fish.

Now the family dissolves. Young and older kingfishers scatter. Each bird will find its own territory. Until the next time of mating each bird will live alone.

22

Diving Deep

Loons are among the most primitive of living birds. They share their grouping with no other. All four modern species are found in North America.

Common loons go to breed on deserted northern lakes. They court among the profuse blooming of water lilies. It is not difficult to recognize these large black and white birds. Their beaks are straight and pointed, necks fairly long and stout, the body sleek and torpedo-shaped. The tails are so short they seem almost missing. Loons have two easily distinguishable calls. One is long, wailing, and plaintive. The second is wild and crazy laughter. From it comes the saying "crazy as a loon."

The sleek but strangely hunched body of the loon cuts the air at speeds up to 60 miles per hour. Its wings are narrow, tapering, and set well back on the body. The wing surface for body weight is the least for any flying bird. With such equipment, becoming airborne is a great problem. Loons that accidentally have alighted on land are doomed. They cannot take off from a dry surface. On the water they must run, paddle, and flap for great distances before rising in the air. Twenty-five yards, fifty, a quarter mile—these birds seem to spatter along endlessly before at last curving up and away from the surface.

In order to nest, loons must leave the water. They build large reedy platforms on lakeshores—and it's hard work. The loons are almost helpless on land. Their legs are encased in the body to the ankle joint, their webbed feet set far back. A few very awkward steps or a slide on the belly are the best they can manage. The word "loon" probably comes from a Scandanavian word *loom*, which means a clumsy person.

Water is the true element of loons. Their bones are not air-filled as

(*Bottom left*) Pacific Loon, (*top left*) Red-throated Loon, (*center*) Greater Common Loon, (*bottom right*) Yellow-billed Loon

those of most birds, but heavy and weighted for swimming. Beneath the lake surface the short wings and almost absent legs are a benefit. Loons are among the best of avian swimmers. They do not "fly" with wings underwater, as do penguins or many other aquatic birds, but their webbed feet propel them rapidly. The wings are used only for balancing and turning. The transparent third eyelid or nictitating membrane acts as a protective lens for underwater swimming.

Like many ducks and grebes, loons have two methods of going underwater. While floating on the surface, they arch the neck, point the beak downward, and with a powerful thrust plunge quickly under. They also may expel air from their air sacs and feathers, then sink gradually beneath the surface.

Although loons do most of their fishing in shallow water, they can dive very deep. One was found trapped in a fisherman's net 240 feet beneath the surface. The average feeding dive is only thirty to forty-five seconds, however. Escape dives may be longer. Loons can stay underwater three to five minutes and travel 300 to 400 yards.

Such long underwater dives are impossible for people. Suffocation or heart failure will kill a human in a few minutes. Within five minutes there is irreversible brain damage from lack of blood circulation.

Loons are like us in their oxygen needs for brain and heart. However, they and other diving birds and mammals can make long underwater jaunts by a special adaptation called bradycardia. Humans have this ability but only to a very slight extent.

As the birds goes underwater, its heart quickly slows to about one-tenth its normal rate. The temperature drops with the lowered metabolism or speed of use of fuel. The body does not heat with activity to so great an extent as it would normally. In addition, the outer portions of the circulatory system close down. The waste products from the muscles are not put into the arteries or veins. Blood circulates only to those organs that can least stand to be without an oxygenated supply. All during the dive the heart and the brain remain well bathed with fresh blood.

23

To the Edge of Extinction

Living things have always become extinct. Our planet is a restless place. A mountain range rises where once the land was flat; the climate goes from cool to hot; ponds dry; a river changes its course. A species that cannot adapt to change dies. New species arise.

Changes in geology and climate are slow; human changes are fast. People increasingly cover the earth. For a long time few cared for other species at all. Many animals were killed for sport or curiosity or greed. Millions of passenger pigeons fell with the crack of guns. The huge breeding colonies of great auk were bludgeoned to extinction. Plume hunters nearly wiped out herons and egrets. At last laws were passed to protect many kinds of wildlife. The senseless greedy killing has stopped, but another kind of destruction rushes on.

Huge cities spread many miles from the center. The once-thick forests are lumbered. Marshes are drained or filled. In such places many birds and other animals once lived and bred. Some of the displaced living things are able to find new places to breed or foods to eat. Others that cannot adapt face a rapidly approaching end.

Unwittingly humans also have poisoned the air, the land, and the water. Much of this has been realized too late. DDT was outlawed in 1971, but its devastating effects continue. The poison is stored in the bodies of worms, fish, or other creatures. Birds that eat them die a quivering, slow death. This is only part of the damage. Eagles and brown pelicans are threatened with extinction because of DDT. The chemical causes the shells of their eggs to be very thin. A great number break before hatching. There are few young to replace the older birds.

Since the last dodo was killed in 1681, seventy-five other types of

NEAR EXTINCTION (*Left*) American Peregrine Falcon, (*right*) American Bald Eagle

EXTINCT NORTH AMERICAN BIRDS (*Top left*) Carolina Parakeet, (*top right*) Passenger Pigeon, (*bottom*) Great Auk

birds have become extinct. Two percent of the world's bird species are presently considered extremely rare. Fifty-three American birds are classified as in close danger of extinction. Rarest of the rare may be the ivory-billed woodpecker.

The ivorybill differs from many of the well-known birds that are now extinct. It never was common. Very early naturalists and collectors realized that these birds were becoming even more scarce. At one time ivorybills lived in the swampy forests of coastal plains from North Carolina to Texas and northward in the Mississippi swamps to Illinois and Oklahoma. By 1891 they were found only in the southernmost portion of the range.

Laws were passed to protect the ivorybills from hunting and egg collecting, but the numbers of birds continued to decrease. By 1926 ivorybills were believed extinct. New hope flared in 1932, when a few birds were found in Louisiana and South Carolina. In 1937 the National Audubon Society paid for a study of these enormous woodpeckers, believing that possibly with more knowledge the ivorybill might be saved.

For several years a man—J. T. Tanner—lived with the woodpeckers and studied their habits. He watched the birds court by touching or clasping bill to bill and exchanging a few low musical notes. He camped beneath the nest holes and watched the babies grow and fledge. He followed the paired male and female as they moved with swift, strong flight on feeding forays that skimmed the tops of trees for miles. The loud call of *kent . . . kent* or double-blow signal pounding on dead trees guided him through the thick forests. In this time he came to know the ivorybill well. Thirty years later his report remains possibly the last intimate portrait of this greatly endangered species.

Conclusions about the ivorybill's future were not very hopeful, and time has shown them to be unfortunately correct. The Cuban race of these woodpeckers was fifteen in 1956, when the last count was taken. The current number of birds is completely unknown. In 1941 there were twenty-four ivorybills reported in the United States. None has been sighted recently, but some may remain in remote areas of Louisiana, Texas, and South Carolina. The hope is not great, however. Many bird lovers and naturalists fear the ivorybill may very well be extinct.

All year the ivorybill lived only in pairs or in family groups. Never did they flock with others of their kind. The bond of male and female was close. The birds stayed near each other while feeding. In deep dry roost holes they spent the nights separately, yet not far apart. Morning began with a preening and stretching in the sunlight. The clear *kent . . . kent . . . kent* call of one bird brought an immediate answer. The male and female left together to feed.

The ivorybill never produced large numbers of eggs. There was one brood of two to three eggs. The nest was well attended. Male and female took turns. Each night the male brooded. During the day the female remained on the eggs. These large colorful woodpeckers often had a nest relief ceremony. The arriving bird called or pounded. The incubating partner came from the nest. The two hung with their strong, curved, sharp woodpecker toes and exchanged a few low musical notes.

The nest was chiseled about twenty inches deep. It was a warm, dry, safe place. The baby birds were fed for two months after leaving the nest, and the family group remained together for many months afterward. Most babies easily grew to maturity. Few creatures other than man preyed upon them.

Before the coming of the whites the ivorybill maintained its numbers. Some of the birds were killed for ornamentation or magic, but there was no danger of extinction. It was not the gun or the arrow that destroyed the ivorybill. The hatchet and the buzzing power saw in the end were the deadliest of the enemies.

When men came into the forests to lumber, there were great changes. Dead and dying trees were no longer allowed to remain, but were cut to make room for the young and healthy. With long barbed tongue, the ivorybill fed on wood borers immediately beneath the bark of newly dead or dying trees. Their major food disappeared with the dead trees. Lumbering spread. Again and again the birds moved away, and their numbers grew less.

No one knows for sure exactly why the birds began to disappear, as well as to retreat from cut areas. Perhaps the parent birds deserted the disturbed nests or trees crashed down with unfeathered young. Perhaps the few birds that remained inbred too much and became sterile. Older birds may have died from starvation or laid fewer eggs because of less food. Fewer and fewer young hatched and reached maturity. As the number of remaining birds grew less, the chances of extinction grew large. A violent storm, a season of disease, the greedy killings of a single poacher—all make little difference to a species with large numbers. But for those with few, such happenings may mark the end.

(Left) Ivory-billed Woodpecker, *(right)* Yellow-shafted Flicker

The decrease of the ivorybill is less spectacular than that of the dodo, the auk, or the passenger pigeon. It is the type of threat that is most real for endangered birds today. As long as we continue to change and destroy the natural world without concern for the results to other living things, many more plants and animals will become threatened, endangered, and at last extinct.

All creatures are linked in the web of life. When we threaten so many, we endanger ourselves.

The Author

Lucille Wood Trost, who holds bachelor and master's degrees in zoology and biology and a PhD in human behavior, is the author of *The Lives and Deaths of a Meadow* and *Biography of a Cottontail* from Putnam's. Mrs. Trost, who lives in Pocatello, Idaho, with her husband and young son, has done medical and biological research, besides writing extensively on nature and wildlife subjects. *The Lives and Deaths of a Meadow* was cited as "an outstanding science book for children."

The Artist

Joseph Sibal is a natural history artist whose work has been widely acclaimed in this country and his native Austria. Among the books he has illustrated for Putnam's are *The Strange World of Sea Mammals*, *Monsters of the Ancient Seas*, *The Strange World of Insects*, *The Amazing Animals of Latin America*, and *The Amazing Animals of Australia*. His paintings were often reproduced in *Life* magazine.

Index